How To Analyze People

The simple guide on understanding the art of reading people, human behavior, personality types, the power of body language, and how to influence others.

Peter Rajon

This eBook, Book is provided with the sole purpose of providing relevant information on a specific topic for which every reasonable effort has been made to ensure that it is both accurate and reasonable. Nevertheless, by purchasing this eBook, you consent to the fact that the author, as well as the publisher, are in no way experts on the topics contained herein, regardless of any claims as such that may be made within. As such, any suggestions or recommendations that are made within are done so purely for entertainment value. It is recommended that you always consult a professional prior to undertaking any of the advice or techniques discussed within.

This is a legally binding declaration that is considered both valid and fair by both the Committee of Publishers Association and the American Bar Association and should be considered as legally binding within the United States.

The reproduction, transmission, and duplication of any of the content found herein, including any specific or extended information will be done as an illegal act regardless of the end form the information ultimately takes. This includes copied versions of the work, both physical, digital, and audio unless the express consent of the Publisher is provided beforehand. Any additional rights reserved.

Furthermore, the information that can be found within the pages described forthwith shall be considered both accurate and truthful when it comes to the recounting of facts. As such, any use, correct or incorrect, of the provided information will render the Publisher free of responsibility as to the actions taken outside of their direct purview. Regardless, there are zero scenarios where the original author or the Publisher can be deemed liable in any fashion for any damages or hardships that may result from any of the information discussed herein.

TABLE OF CONTENTS

INTRODUCTION

Congratulations on purchasing How to Analyze People and Understand the Human Mind and thank you for doing so.

The following chapters will discuss the art of reading the human mind and peeking into their personality in a subtly effective way. The human personality is like a jigsaw puzzle; it has a complete set pattern to be followed. The puzzle should be put together by joining the missing pieces in such a way that each piece is fitted perfectly into its corresponding place. The set-provided pattern acts as a photo image or a prompt to match the pieces accordingly, almost like a comprehensive analysis. This book helps you better understand the way of performing that analysis. The person analyzing the human personality may realize that the behavior patterns, the motivational factors, the color preferences, the body language, and the verbal communication styles, etc. are all important indicators of an individual's personality.

When you are learning the art of behavioral analysis and speed-reading people, you should be able to understand that observation is vital to analyzing people. It is key to opening the door of hidden character traits, behaviors, and emotions that were quite unnoticed before due to a lack of tactful observation. To be able to perceive your subject's personality and speed-read his mind, you should able to adopt techniques that will help you not only better capable of understanding his intentions, words, and actions, but also let you influence his mind. In this book, there are 33 actionable techniques mentioned that can be learned and practiced systematically in the span of just 5 weeks. Let's learn them!

There are plenty of books on this subject on the market, thanks again for choosing this one! Every effort was made to ensure it is full of as much useful information as possible, and please enjoy it!

CHAPTER 1: IMPORTANCE OF ANALYZING PEOPLE AND UNDERSTANDING THE HUMAN MIND

People often think that the easiest way to understand the human mind is by studying your own mind. However, the fact is that the human mind is a complex bundle of entangled nerves and feelings. Even if it is your own mind, you have to delve deeper and work harder to understand the underlying intricacies of your cognition. On the other hand, when it comes to understanding someone else's mind, the process requires seemingly difficult yet systematically easy techniques to follow, which can eventually lead to an understandable pattern of human mind analysis.

Humans are interesting beings with astonishing mind powers, functioning abilities, and responses. The more we dig, the more we come up with unveiled facts and layers of the mind. The memories, the past experiences, the learned lessons, the emotional chaos, the relational feelings, and each and every bit of life's practicalities are etched on the mind.

No matter what the circumstances are and who the

confronter of these circumstances is, the mind has a response to each particular stimulus that is presented by the situation at hand. This sort of reactivity makes the human mind prone to dynamic changes and psychological conditioning. It also makes a person unique from his other contemporaries. The variable quality of the human mind is quite similar to how unique each person's impressions are from the other. From afar, each of them may seem to have more or less the same nose, pair of eyes, ears, and the same number of fingers. However, when one observes carefully and comes to have a closer look, the uniqueness unfolds.

Experts suggest that human mental structures are different from each other in their wiring and conditioning because there are several factors influencing humans. People shape their minds according to the factors related to their environment, culture, society, work ethics, and tradition. To understand the workings of people's minds, we must first get to know these influential factors ranging from psychological, emotional, physical, and moral domains to professional, relational, lingual, and societal aspects.

Human society is a combination of differentially, unique beings. They cohabit, interact, and build up relationships. There is always a curious aspect lingering under the initiative of interaction. The interaction becomes fun when it stoops to the same level and frequency of mental chemistry. The communication at both ends become fluent, less awkward, and more interesting. On the other hand, if the communicators are not in sync due to their opinion differences or lack of familiarity with each other, or difference in mental levels, the interaction would be quite awkward and boring. This usually happens when practical strangers from different backgrounds come in contact and try to interact without properly knowing each other's mindset. Contrarily, without interaction, it would have been difficult to know a person and analyze the human mind.

When it comes to human behavioral analysis, it means to consider a person as your subject of study. It may sound quite mechanical and materialistic, but rest assured that there are more feelings involved in this than you imagine. Every single bit of the brain is an emotional rollercoaster of feelings and thoughts.

The mind works the way it feels. - I. F.

To survive in this society and to do it successfully, one must possess an awareness of not just his own self but the people he lives with and meet frequently or might have a chance to meet in the future. Awareness is such a deep, enlightening concept. If we study it, we understand that it is not just an internal process; instead, it involves the internal sensory perception and an external acquisition of information. This information coming from external via internal sensory perceptive organs acting as windows of awareness gets to be interpreted by cognitive receptors and output as comprehensive knowledge.

How gratifying would that be if, in this huge world, peace, love, and mutual understanding could prevail due to the avoidance of possible conflicts, clash of opinions, antagonism, and several misunderstandings? This avoidance can be possible by gaining not only self-awareness but also people's awareness. Howard Gardiner has named this sort of awareness as being people smart. Many would name it as emotional intelligence, too. The concept of EQ, however, will be discussed in detail in the later chapter of this book. For now, let us imagine how people must become intelligent in analyzing themselves and their fellow beings to make this world more livable. The world could become a happy place of friendly dwellers if all sorts of conflicts could be resolved due to being aware of the strengths and shortcomings of your fellows, their thoughts and actions, and of their motives and intentions. This is in no way being judgmental; it is readily aware of how you or any other person may behave in a given situation. It is possible; it is achievable. The term utopia would not be just for an imaginary concept. Similarly, people would be eager to sort out their potential problems and issues on the basis of this state of harmony and understanding. This may seem quite a far-fetched notion, but at least we can start from somewhere.

"Little drops of rain can make the mighty ocean." When Julia Abigail Fletcher Carney wrote this amazingly true verse, she actually tried to convey the importance of small efforts made by each living individual which can eventually combine together to make a noticeable difference.

Experts believe that the possibility to bring a change begins with an effort to alter the dynamics of the world you live or the action frame of your everyday life. You may have heard the phrase "thinking outside the box." Let us alter it a bit for you by phrasing it as tailor the box to fit the thought in. This happens when you are constantly on the move, thinking solutions, analyzing the work patterns, and thinking behaviors. This happens when you realize how crucial it is to interpret what people think, say, and do. This happens when how they behave starts to influence you as well, whether in the short run or long run eventually. This realization takes you on the route to discovering the secrets of the human mind, unearthing the complex thoughts, and understanding the behavioral patterns that not only shape an individual's mental schemas but also collectively form a public mindset, influencing the overall demographics. The mental schemes are not a set criterion box. They are not static; they are not fixed. There is always some sort of accommodation or assimilation taking place. You should understand the structural dynamics and the logical changes that are taking place in the box of your mind and be able to tailor that box according to these changes.

Suppose you meet a person who is a practical stranger to you, what can you do to break the ice in between? How will you start a conversation? Which topic will you choose? These questions are all quite dynamic in nature. Just like the dynamic nature of the human mind, human interactions are also quite unique from person to person. Maybe you are stuck with a person in a train's compartment for a long journey spanning hours. The silence, although speaks a lot when no one is speaking, becomes overwhelmingly burdensome after a while. That person is observing you by throwing subtle glances your way. You are also doing the same when he is not doing it. How do you think your glances will help you analyze him? The results may vary according to the techniques you are keeping in mind while analyzing him. What does his posture tell you? What are his facial expressions while being silent? Does he seem expressive enough? Does he seem like a stoic person? If he starts to speak, what sort of results can you deduce by his way of talking, choice of words, and voice intonation? Can you predict what will be his next action before he actually does it? Can you read his thoughts and foretell what will be his next words before he actually speaks them? Interestingly, if he is observant enough, he may be doing the same as you are doing without letting you realize him analyzing you.

This subtle perception and personality analysis are actually an inevitable part of our life. Even if a person is quite untrained in the art of human behavioral classification and mind-reading, he still consciously or unconsciously pays attention to certain things. Without even realizing this, he automatically notices his cohabiters, his friends, his surroundings, his subordinates, and his own reactions to their stimulating actions or their reactions to his own actions. The people are all a part of a beaded chain interlinked together. A nudge in a particular direction will cause a bead to move and nudge the adjacent one until all of them are moving and passing through the thread. If one of them is stuck in the way, it will become a hurdle in harmonious flow and movement. Similarly, the ripple effect in the waterworks.

Most of us have experience in playing stone skipping. Upon throwing the flat stone into the water bed, mostly, your eyes are focused on the stone to follow the number of bounces. However, the alternative way to look at this or the other side of the picture will be to focus on the water that has been subjected to the ripple effect. How interestingly, one circular wave pattern nudges the other, and that other one touches another until an influential pattern is formed that starts inwardly and expands outwardly. This effect is a clear message to us analyzers that just like the stone causing multiple ripples in the water, an action or behavior of a person can also be continuously influential and crucial in several given situations.

You must have heard countless times the saying: Think before you act. But the truth there is far more to this statement that just thinking and doing. Aligning your intention with your action is just not enough. Instead, you must align your intention with the possible outcome of your action. Here you think what actually does it mean? Confused? Don't be! It simply means to predict how a person you are addressing your words to will possibly behave in response to those words and how your intended actions can affect him. This can be mastered by understanding human personality analysis.

The human mind, as a subject of study, makes an interesting book for reading if one is a bibliophile. However, even if you aren't an avid reader, it can still prove to be an exhilarating ride to experience. In this book, you can imagine a book within a book! We shall be discussing some of those concepts that serve as chapters of the book of the human mind along with the consequent benefits of speed-reading people, psychological intricacies of the organ called mind, and the relationship between mind, body, and actions.

CHAPTER 2: BENEFITS OF ANALYZING PEOPLE AND BASICS OF HUMAN BEHAVIORAL PSYCHOLOGY

Personality is a fascinating concept in human behavioral psychology. While behavior defines the actions and manners of a person, personality itself is a collection of those behaviors. You can say that behavior is a building block of personality. The human personality is a unique set of characteristic traits, thinking patterns, and actions. Each individual has a specific set of behaviors that distinguishes him from his counterparts. The behavioral psychologists and personality development experts have classified several types of human personality according to individual differences and unique trait patterns that emerge together as a unified whole forming a persona.

According to research, paradigms are behaviors set of conceptual thoughts that help us identify a person's habits and the motivation behind his actions. Then this paradigm can sometimes experience either a sudden or a more gradual shift that reconditions the entire thought process of an individual. A question might arise that why should we, while analyzing people, try to see their point of view? The answer to this question leads to our changed attitude towards public dealing. Each individual possessing individual thoughts, is, in fact, also a participant of a global thought process.

Psychology is a science that may seem quite clichéd to most people but is actually a very layered scientific domain. It deals with various real yet abstract concepts that may seem complex at the surface, but once studied in a systematic manner, it can lead to more concrete approaches. Behavioral psychology is also a part of a much wider domain, and itself has many subdomains. It is closely linked to cognitive psychology and deals with concepts such as behavior, learning, stimulus, response, reinforcements, habit formation, environment, mental schemas, conditioning, and cognitive reprogramming.

If a person aims to be successful in life, his ambition alone will not be enough. Numerous hindrances may occur in his path to the successful accomplishment of the desired goals and objectives in life. This is because we don't live in a crystal ball isolated from others. We are a social animal. Socialization is our breathing lifeline. We cannot expect the life's path to be linear and one dimensional in a way that nothing crosses us while traveling that path. The fact is that each person's pathway in life intersects or connects at some point with other pathways. At that point, one needs to be well prepared for facing the world and its people. It is vitally important to be able to analyze how people think, act, and react and to be able to understand what they intend, plan, and expect. This benefits us in achieving not only our own objectives but also clearing the path for someone else too. It may be termed as some sort of symbiotic relationship in humans.

The key to success is an appropriate paradigm shift, and the key to shifting your paradigm or someone else's is to understand people in general. Public smartness is key to a successful approach towards goal setting and action planning. It is also instrumental in effective communication and socialization.

Think hard, why would people want to be remembered by someone, and why would you want to remember them?

It is mainly because of the fact that a particularly striking trait of their behavior catches your eye and remains in your mind for quite a long time.

People tend to stereotype others by typecasting them into fixed categories. However, to see a person standing out in a crowd, we must seem to understand that particular, striking quality of an individual that sets him apart from others. Your old friends from school will be forever remembered by you, even if you have made dozens of newer friends in both college and professional life. Not just because they were dearer to you, but also because you spent more time with them, paid more attention to them, and each one of the group was known for some of their striking, unique traits. Maybe it was a nosy attitude of Anna, or a lazy persona of Tyler, or an untidy appearance of Sam, or loud laughter of Ben. All of these were memorable traits that distinguished them, so they remained in your mind for a long time.

Now, coming towards your newer friends, you may also be able to understand and remember them if you were truly interested, but the point here is not just to remember for the sake of memory. The point is, to be able to understand them in order to shape your own attitude towards them in a constructive manner until they respond to you in the same manner. This is also called behavioral conditioning or public programming.

This concept also becomes greatly beneficial in the business and professional arena. Recruitment, retention, and appraisals, etc. are all a part of a professional employment routine. There is a whole branch of business administration dedicated to people management called Human Resource management. The HR department deals with the tasks mentioned above and much more regularly, and job analysis is a big part of it. The job analysis not only helps organizations in the determination of suitable employee choices for a particular role, but it also helps them study in detail the potential candidates' behavior, abilities, mindset, and expected work outcomes. The interviews are also a major tool in determining the most suitable candidate among the applicants by analyzing them and understanding their work objectives, ambitions, perception, and ethics.

The human personality analysis has become so influential in taking major decisions in various aspects of life that experts nowadays are emphasizing more on the importance of soft, life skills and emotional intelligence than on academic achievements and high grades. This may be because now, people are gaining awareness on how living successfully and surviving in practical scenarios is more important than just attending schools to gain formal, idealistic education. Confronting the practicality of life needs one to remove the rose-tinted glasses from the eyes. To see the world experientially, one must realize the interdependence of its dwellers on each other. Though, this was not the case centuries back. In primitive ages, the humans were quite caught up in their own isolated living area. There were seldom any interactions or communication. No particular language was operational. The basics such as eating, sleeping, hunting, and protecting, etc. were the main daily activities in order to survive. We can say that humans were indeed just starting to climb Maslow's Pyramid of human needs or the Hierarchy of Human Motivation. The first step in the pyramid is the need for fulfillment of the basic physiological necessities such as air, shelter, food, clothing, sleep, etc. That is what primitive man did and require.

However, now that the times have evolved, humans have become more civilized and intellectualized. They have learned to make protective shelters, modern buildings, and health maintenance centers for themselves. They have learned to lighten the darkness and darken the light with just a click of a switch. They have learned to speak several languages in order to communicate for the sake of cohabitation, trading, teaching, learning, writing, and simply understanding each other. They have continued to climb higher in the hierarchy, and there are certain motivations that seem to be the driving force in pursuing the fulfillment of each stage of the needs.

Whether it be physical or physiological, security or safety, love and belonging, esteem, or self-actualization, each stage comprises a set of human needs that are driven by certain motivations in order to be fulfilled.

CHAPTER 3: OBSERVATION, RECOGNITION, AND EVALUATION

Analyzing the people proves to be quite enjoyable and informative if followed in an organized pattern. The process has a path paved with some proposed milestones. Reaching them can ensure the successful journey of learning people's behavior and reading their minds. Embarking on this journey, the three components of the initial milestone are observation, recognition, and evaluation.

Observation:

Imagine yourself as a microscope, the world being your subject of study. How many wondrous revelations can you unveil by just observing carefully and closely? Experts view that every human upon birth is bestowed with a special kind of mental power to observe and explore the surroundings. A baby's mind has this innate ability to take in impressions from the environment and absorb them. This observational absorption of information occurs initially at an unconscious stage but soon transforms into a conscious effort on an individual's part. This way, not only mental muscles are created, but also the observational mentality becomes operational.

At an early age, the mind is so special that the acquisition of knowledge occurs naturally. Listening to sounds, touching surfaces, smelling fragrances, etc. These small sensory actions can make an individual literate in the workings of the world he lives in. However, afterward, the concentration and conscious effort begin to play a vital role in making this knowledge more comprehensible and more profoundly meaningful. Observation, at its best, can be an instrument for gaining insightful knowledge. Using that knowledge, one can derive conclusions that facilitate growth and development in a holistic manner.

Recognition:

As time passes, a person becomes more informed and knowledgeable about his environment. He begins to recognize things and identify them. This stage of recognition is quite influential. It can make or break a concept and shift the mental paradigm completely. However, this recognition concept is closely dependent on existing mental schemas and preset wiring of the brain. A person recognizes an old thing as he has perceived it before. Or he recognizes a new thing mostly based on his perception of similar looking things.

A kid, upon seeing a cat, is told that it is called a cat and it has four legs. Now, upon seeing another animal with four legs that he has never seen before, he is likely to call it a cat, too. This is because the first time he saw a cat, his mind took an impression and saved it. A mental structure was formed, adding or storing this knowledge in the brain. The second time a stimulating image of a similar-looking animal was shown to him, the mind combed through previous knowledge to come up with possible explanation or name for the new image. Thus what the brain stores in there, is what the brain represents again and again unless a new schema is formed or an older one gets adjusted to the newer information. This is what we call mental reprogramming. So, when the observer is taking notice of his surrounding environment or meets people, he is likely to form opinions and recognize different signs and behaviors. This recognition would be according to his mental conditioning unless he learns techniques to analyze people in a systematic manner.

Evaluation:

The third stage is Evaluation. As the name suggests, to evaluate means to asses, analyze, and form an idea about a thing or concept. The word "analyze" cannot be interchangeably used with evaluating because both of them have some distinguishing features that define them. Analysis means to break a whole into parts and study these parts to understand the whole. Evaluation means to determine or estimate the significance of a concept. Mostly, after the observation and recognition of a concept or behavior, the observer analyzes it by interpreting each part carefully and then evaluate it by realizing and determining the impact and significance of each part of the observed behavior or incident. The evaluation helps in deriving the results and reaching to possible conclusions and explanations. It can also give way to post-observational reflections and realizations. By following the implications suggested by an effective evaluation, an observer is led to an improved personality change and behavioral positivity. In theory, evaluation should be an unbiased judgment. However, experts recommend the observation should be unbiased, based on factually objective data while evaluation can be a personal assessment of that data.

Week 1

Let us start our first week of understanding the basics of analyzing people by learning the first three techniques, as mentioned below.

TECHNIQUE 1: OBSERVING THE SURROUNDINGS

Experts in behavioral psychology say that one of the most troublesome hindrances faced by mankind in leading a successful life today is an appropriate reaction to corresponding stimuli. The surroundings you live in may seem quite familiar to you in a way that you tend to lose interest in observing them. Eventually, it becomes a habit, and even if you go somewhere else, to an unfamiliar place, your lack of observational curiosity catches up to you there as well. However, you must understand that you have to build this habit in you to observe places, people, objects, vehicles, etc. anything that constitutes the environment surrounding you or the person you intend to analyze. The first technique is to just perceive and observe. Looking is to notice something; seeing or perceiving is to notice it intelligently; observing is to not only noticing it but taking notes as well, i.e., recording it or retaining it in mind carefully.

While performing observation, the observer must be patient and persevering. Accurateness and attention is the key to gather productive information. Be careful about noticing the details in order to avoid missing even a single nuance. Sometimes, a little bit of change in one's behavior can be a root cause of action, and people not keen on their observations often tend to miss or overlook that exact particular change. Try to avoid being that careless observer if you want to be successful in your analysis.

The following action steps will summarize this technique more comprehensively:

✓ Select a subject of study, i.e., a person whom you intend to analyze.
✓ Keep in mind the goal of your observation. An aimless observation mostly serves as a distraction and a cognitive traffic jammer, instead of being a purposeful activity.
✓ Concentrate, as it is the key to gathering sufficient information through observation. When you are concentrating on the person, you zero your sensory powers on him, indicating to the brain how important this analysis is to you. Therefore, the brain exercises its

full potential in noticing things about the subject.

✓ Keep in mind the preliminary data or background information, if possible. However, an observation from scratch can also be useful in the case of practical strangers.

✓ Pursue your task at hand with singular obsession, i.e., don't multi-task at this time. Just be calm and pay attention. Calmness helps in increasing the focus and saves the energy as a back up to be used.

✓ Be as objective as you can in order to form an independent perspective.

✓ Make sure the observation is as subtle as possible. You don't want to be labeled as a stalker or staring freak. Remember, you are the one who is noticing, not the one being noticed.

✓ Consider all the possible sources of information while performing the observation.

✓ Keep in mind that, although, the methods may be quite similar to scientific observation, observing people can be a bit prejudicial even if only in an unconscious way. This can be avoided by consciously clearing your mind from previous stereotypes and biases.

TECHNIQUE 2: RECOGNIZING THE ENVIRONMENTAL FACTORS

The second technique is recognizing environmental factors. The surrounding environment of a person you mean to analyze is actually a maze that hides several unearthed traits. Once you begin to observe closely, you feel a certain curiosity to explore and recognize things in a meaningful manner in order to understand each thing's purpose and functionality. Also, this recognition will help you understand how a certain person behaves and why he does so. The environment has a close relationship with the psychology of the human mind. Environmental psychology is a whole branch of psychological sciences dedicated to the relationship between living organisms and their surrounding environment. As mentioned previously, a human being is not an isolated creature manufactured as a standalone book. It is just one book in a huge chain of books. Then these books are arranged on different shelves located in different book stores. To determine the exact location and situational setting of a particular piece, you have to closely observe and explore the surroundings.

Mainly any environment has two types of factors that influence the people living there. These factors are either external or internal in nature. Both of these factors are instrumental in impacting an individual and his surrounding environment. External environmental factors include economic, social, educational, climatic, geographic, technical, media, etc. These are also called outer influencers. Whereas, the internal environmental factors or influencers include moral values, cultural norms, and traditions, motivations, attitudes, and beliefs, etc.

A person is greatly influenced by these factors. A deep look into the culture of a community or society will let us know about the common beliefs, habits, and expected behaviors of the people residing there. Further observation and recognition of the influence of media sources such as newspapers, journals, books, internet websites and portals, radio and television channels, will let us know changes that may have occurred in the demographics of a particular region. The mindset change occurs when these factors are present in the environment. The trick is to keep these in mind while analyzing a person. Also, the constant practice can help you recognize these elemental influencers that work in the background more quickly.

- ✓ Recognize how the social setting is shaped and how the person you are analyzing gels or fits in.
- ✓ Recognize the climate and geographic setting of the place.
- ✓ Recognize the educational, economic, and emotional background of the person.
- ✓ Recognize the influence of technology, print, and social media on the dwellers in an area.
- ✓ Recognize the school of thought or belief to which a person you are analyzing belongs.
- ✓ Recognize the cultural differences and moral values that might affect a person's outlook.
- ✓ Remember that all the recognized factors can be crucial to your analysis in one way or the other. Don't underestimate the importance of any one of them.
- ✓ Review once again and make sure that the subject person indeed seems to belong to that particular environment

of which you have recognized the factors.

The above action steps will be fruitful in making use of the observational efforts you made following the first technique and will help in progressing with the third technique.

TECHNIQUE 3: EVALUATING THE TRAITS AND OTHER IMPACTS

This technique involves the detailed assessment of environmental factors that you have recognized before. As the process of evaluation ensures that the gathered information is categorized systematically and understood for its impactful significance, the determination of the impact of each one of the environmental influencers on an individual is important. This can be ensured by first examining each recognized factor in detail. Understanding its range, capacity, and power of influence is vital to determine its significance.

For example, after observing a person's surroundings and environmental situation carefully, you recognized an externally influential factor, i.e., education. Now, the action step is to delve deeper into the impact of this factor on that particular person. Determine how it might be affecting his behavior, speech, and action. How and what capacity of behavioral change and personality improvement is possible due to this factor, i.e., acquiring education. To what extent or range has he actually been successful in gaining the education and how much time he has spent in doing so. These assessed facts can change your perspective about a person, and this can help you in understanding them better because you become more aware of their intellectual speech, or from where they are coming from while seeming to be pretentious at first glance.

Consider another, more practical example; while you are observing a person, you recognize that he is quite averse to eating with a spoon or fork, etc. You recognize that he belongs to a particular culture where eating with the hand is preferred. While evaluating these facts and their impact, you may reach to a more positive conclusion that the significantly different culture has prompted this behavior consciously or unconsciously rather than lack of table manners. Therefore, it becomes apparent that people should be analyzed, keeping these factors in mind. If these techniques are practiced at the initial phase of your journey, you will be better capable to aptly take notice of individual differences that are vital in shaping the person's thoughts and behaviors.

To summarize the action steps for the technique of evaluation, consider these points:

✓ After recognition of both the external and internal influencers, make sure to delimitate the subject's surroundings so that your mind doesn't wander around unmarked territories.

✓ Refresh the recognized information in mind.

✓ Reflect on the gathered information. Reflection is the essence of observation. There can be no possibility of improvement and development, nor can there be solutions or conclusions without practicing the art of reflection. The reflection explores questions like what happened, how it happened, why did it happen or what does it mean, and what might this implicate for the future?

✓ Analyze the factors by decoding the collective

information into chunks and assessing each one's relationship with the person separately.

✓ Design sub-questions. Reflection can be more systematic if followed by properly designing the underlying questions to ask and enquire such as how could social media have impacted the person in question, or why does a person prefer to sit down on the floor instead of on the chair? or what level of economic/financial difficulty might have forced this highly experienced person to seek entry-level employment? There can be a long list of possible scenarios and questions that may be developed to analyze and evaluate a person's behavior.

✓ Create a strategic process for seeking answers to these questions such as meeting, communicating, and discussing.

✓ Derive results and conclude the information.

✓ Compliment your evaluated information by personal statements or perspective.

CHAPTER 4: BEHAVIOR, MOTIVATION, AND PERSONALITY

In previous chapters, the definition of behavior and personality was mentioned. In this chapter, we will discuss the relationship of these with another important component of human psychology, i.e., motivation. Motivation defines the reason or cause of the action of an individual. It also happens to be the driving force behind each goal a person sets, or each struggle he undergoes to achieve the desired object. Without the motivational push, an individual's behaviors are in a state of chaos, so the personality also becomes confused and disoriented. The root word of motivation is motive meaning a certain need to accomplish something.

Psychology experts say that humans are controlled by their own minds unless they learn to control it themselves. The needs, desires, and wishes are the one that guides our actions. We become a slave to them if we follow them blindly and obligingly. The personality becomes controlled and submissive to these compulsive urges. To understand this, consider an example of a street boy who has no money to pay for the cheeseburger he so craves. There is a nearby stall where a vendor is selling hot, yummy cheeseburgers. The boy is passing by the stall, in his ragged appearance. Initially, he attempts to come and beg for his desirous food, but the vendor tells him off in a sneering manner. Now, if he becomes a slave to his hunger, he might submit to the need to steal or deceive.

Analyzing his behavior, we may not subject his whole personality to be of a thief, but we may name this particular behavior like stealing, on a superficial inspection at least. However, still, we cannot say that his motive was to steal. Instead, for him, this served as a means to an end. We are not here to justify his actions, of course, but a possible explanation can be given to explore his underlying motivation to do what he did. Remember, analysis is to understand the behavior rather than justify it, though an explanation and looking deeper into other's perspectives unveils contrary beliefs and personality traits that defy one's apparent actions or behaviors.

Some behavioral psychologists may explain motivation as an impulsive thought or notion. Montessori theory suggests that home is always present in the sub-conscience of the human mind. A person's will to perform an action sometimes gets intercepted by hormetic impulses. A sudden motivation to exhibit a particular behavior can expose the inner desires of an individual's mind. Most people are quite secretive and expressionless. By predicting the possible motivation behind their actions, one can follow their behavioral pattern. This can help in locating the behaviors that may occur, reoccur, or never occur according to the situational need. In a given circumstance, if your subject did a certain action or reacted in a certain way, what sort of need possessed him to do it? What could be his motive? What is the possibility that he may react in a similar manner if he finds himself in the same situation again, plus or minus, any factor? These questions can be answered if closer attention is paid to the relationship between the behavior, motivation, and personality of an individual.

Week 2:

So, dear reader, have you reviewed and practiced the techniques mentioned throughout the previous week? If yes, it is time for proceeding to the next week's techniques. If no, now is your chance to go back a few pages and refresh what you read previously. So without further ado, let us start our second week with some fresh techniques.

TECHNIQUE 4: RECORDING THE BEHAVIOR PATTERN

After understanding the basics of the relationship between the behavior, personality, and motivation, the main step is to record the pattern in which behavior is occurring. As we have briefly mentioned an example of behavior and personality traits previously, we will focus more on the active aspect of behavior patterns here both in theory and practice.

The research experts in the field of psychological behaviorism suggest several special patterns to classify certain behaviors. Some argue that behavioral psychology is quite different from cognitive psychology in the sense that the former is based on the theory of behavior change with respect to the experiences of an individual. While the latter suggests that the behaviors are cognitive reactions to sensory impulses and can be processed and reprocessed according to the cognitive functionality, willpower, and determination of the human mind. The behaviorists emphasize that the behavior pattern is entirely dependent on the external stimulus while cognitive psychologists argue that the behavior pattern can be defined by the way knowledge is encoded, stored, and processed in our cognition. However, to make it simple and applicable, both theories are two different angles of the same picture, i.e., a behavior pattern forms when an individual responds to an external stimulus using his internal senses gains experience, learns things, stores them in his mind, and reiterates his action in a similar, recurring situation.

When we go for a shopping trip, we observe many different shops in the market. Among them are dress shops, jewelry shops, book shops, shoe shops, pharmacies, nurseries, bakeries, grocery shops, etc. If you enter one of them, you are directed to aisles of organized items displayed with proper classification of each category they belong to. For instance, dresses are arranged according to their color, size, structure, and price. If you choose a particular dress, you do so according to your taste. Your taste is defined by your personality. Just like that, your behaviors shaping your personality are also classified and defined by your motivational instinct that, due to recurrence, evolves into a habitual pattern.

• If you wear white, formal dresses on Fridays at work, your particular clothing style becomes your habit displaying a recurring behavior.

• If a student is late in the class for the first time, it may look like an exceptional scenario. However, if he is late every day, he forms a pattern of tardiness which is a type of behavior.

• If a writer researches a topic for the first time, then writes the content, he would not be called a vigorous researcher. Research is a type of behavior. A series of similar research actions performed in succession in order to create each informative piece of content in a consistent manner may exhibit a behavioral pattern and thus, a writer can be called a researcher, too.

Observational psychologists use multiple tools to record behavioral patterns. These tools may include event sampling, time sampling, rubrics, checklists, running records, anecdotal records, portfolios, performance charts, action memos, etc.

Some people interested in analyzing the behavior sets often use customized graphs and legends to records the reactions and responses of a person being observed. Audio recordings, pictures, and other media tools may also help in this regard.

TECHNIQUE 5: DECODING THE MOTIVATION (INTRINSIC + EXTRINSIC)

This technique involves the action step of decoding and evaluating the motivational factors working behind the scenes. Each one of them plays a vital role in dictating a particular set of actions. The term extrinsic refers to the external motivational factors, while the term intrinsic is dedicated to the internal factors of motivation.

The concept of rewards and punishment seems to be closely related to the motivational factors governing an individual's personality. The well-known theory of behavioral psychology called operant conditioning is based on the philosophy of reinforcements or consequences.

A reinforcement is basically a motivational reward to

reinforce or strengthen the desired behavior so that it is repeatedly occurring in a consistent manner. It can be either positive or negative. In positive reinforcement, some desired stimulus or motivational factor is added to generate an intended behavior. Whereas, in negative reinforcement, some undesired stimulus or demotivating factor is taken away or removed in order to generate intended behavior.

✓ For instance, examine how an employee is conditioned to perform well in the presence of a dangling motivation of getting a promotion or a salary raise. Here, good work performance is the intended behavior and the rise in salary or offer of a promotion is the positive reinforcement (something that is going to be given instead of being taken away, to ensure the repetition of similar behavior).

✓ Now, consider a similar scenario in the context of negative reinforcement. An employee is working in an organization that has set some rewards for good work performance. If a person performs well and his work meets the quality standards in a consistent manner, some of his weekly quota of tasks will be lessened to take away the burden. Here, the intended behavior is the same, i.e., good work performance, but right now, it is strengthened or reinforced by removing or taking away an undesired factor, i.e., workload from the person.

Similarly, behavior patterns can also be analyzed by the consequences or the punishing factors that serve as demotivators. If a particular behavior is weakened and not occurring again, it may be because there is some fear of punishment or consequence. Learners are often trained to obey by this sort of operant conditioning. The consequences, too, can be both negative or positive. The rule is the same. If a particularly undesired behavior is recurring in an individual, and its pattern should be weakened, a punishment acts as a stimulus. If an undesired object is added or given to the individual as a punishment to inhibit the bad behavior, it is called positive punishment. If, however, a desired outcome or object is removed or taken away from an individual in an attempt to punish or weaken his resolve so that the bad behavior does not occur again, it is called negative punishment.

✓ For instance, you are analyzing a student, and you have recorded his behavior pattern. Whenever there is a possibility of extra lessons as a punishment for making noise in the class, he becomes obediently silent. This is actually positive punishment because here, an undesired stimulus, i.e., extra lessons, is added to weaken or inhibit an unrequired or bad behavioral pattern (making noise).

✓ Similarly, the same student is motivated to inhibit his undesirable behavior by taking away his desired activity or stimulus, i.e., play period or recess time. In this case, the punishment would be called as negative punishment.

The possibility of these consequences or rewards may motivate or stimulate a person to act or react in a particular behavioral pattern. To exhibit a good or generally desired behavior, an individual can be motivated by extrinsic factors such as:

- Monetary incentives
- Promotional offers

- Encouragement
- Complimentary rewards
- Honors and Certificates
- Appreciation statements
- Performance grading
- Appraisals and applause
- Claps and Badges
- Material gifts
- Greeting cards
- Consolation prizes
- Trophies and medals
- Fame and popularity
- Good reputation, etc.

Whereas, the intrinsic motivational factors are generally related to internal, intangible feelings, emotions, thoughts, and objectives that are governed by your own mind. They may have some interdependency on the extrinsic factors but are mostly personal in nature. The internal drive or urge to succeed, prove yourself, or internal fears can be counted as intrinsic impulses. The positive and negative intrinsic factors of motivation are basically reciprocal of each other. For instance, a person may be motivated by his determination to complete the work on time, or he may be motivated by his lack of determination, to procrastinate. The major intrinsic motivational factors are listed below. Imagine the opposite of each one of them in a contrasting scenario.

- Internal satisfaction
- Enjoyment
- Intention
- Wishes and desires
- Curiosity
- Purpose
- Passion
- Self-confidence (or lack of it)
- Determination (or lack of it)
- Personality growth
- Knowledge acquisition
- Autonomy and freedom
- Love or a sense of belonging
- Compassion
- Security and shelter
- Hunger

- Dedication

- Commitment

- Promise

- Guilt

- Self-consciousness

- Distress

- Sleepiness

- Hesitation

- Complexes such as inferiority or superiority complex,

etc.

After decoding the particular motivation factors that are involved in the exhibition of a specific behavioral pattern, you can be able to understand the triggering elements that govern the personality of an individual. You can apply this technique on various subjects, practicing throughout the week, and progressing on your journey about analyzing people.

TECHNIQUE 6: UNDERSTANDING THE PERSONALITY MODEL

This technique is the final one in this week's action steps. The time for understanding the personality model has come. Till now, we were practicing the single bits and pieces of the personality that is the behavior and its patterns. However, after a thorough understanding of behaviors and how the motivations behind each of them can impact an individual, the personality, as a whole, is to be understood.

First, let us know some more about the background of the personality models theory. In the past, there were many theories about personality traits and classifying them into models of identifiable behavior was a subject of constant study by psychologists. The more researches emerged, the more transition occurred in the explanation of personality models. The verbal factor analysis became quite a tool to classify and define specific personality traits and categorize them as regular models. Several studies were conducted until recent years when finally, this theory became more simplified and applicable. Even though there are some other personality models prevalent, this one has a more verbal and simpler approach, so we will be discussing this particular model under technique number 6. Known as the Big-Five-

Traits personality set or Five-Factor Model (FFM), this set of carefully picked traits comprises of 5 different broad personality aspects. They are named as OCEAN:

- O for Openness
- C for Conscientiousness
- E for Extraversion
- A for Agreeableness
- N for Neuroticism

Each of these trait names is actually named after the verbal descriptors for five vast domains or dimensions of human behavior and psyche. These traits have two sub-aspects each, depicting two extremes in a person's behavior.

These extremes can be stated as:

- Openness (to experience) = Curious or Inventive v/s Cautious or Consistent
- Conscientiousness = Organized or Efficient v/s Careless or Easy-going
- Extraversion = Energetic or Outgoing v/s Reserved

or Solitary

- Agreeableness = Compassionate or Friendly v/s Detached or Challenging
- Neuroticism = Confident or Secure v/s Nervous or Sensitive

This model is based on the verbal descriptor analysis method in which a selected set of descriptive words having related meanings can be used to describe a personality verbally, yet still managing to paint a visual picture of the behavioral patterns exhibited by it.

✓ In the above categories, the word openness (to experience) describes the willingness to learn experientially, explore new things, and create or generate new concepts and ideas. It explains an open, welcoming attitude that portrays a broadminded, revolutionary outlook of a person in his life.

For instance, an individual who is open to experience may possess traits like curiosity, industriousness, inventiveness, revolution, progressiveness, pragmatism, innovation, mobility, radicalism, creativity, spontaneity, and inquisitiveness. Similarly, the person who is not open to experience may possess traits like cautiousness, conservativeness, wariness to unfamiliar concepts, consistency, regularity, predictability, repetitiveness, stagnation, uniformity, etc. You can identify similar word patterns and descriptors in each category mentioned above and understand how the two extremes work in contrast, shaping the two sorts of personality models among the people.

✓ The word conscientiousness means to be organized, diligent, efficient, meticulous, careful, guarded, detailed, attentive, dedicated, punctual, principled, thorough, etc. The lack of this would portray a personality possessing traits such as carelessness, inefficiency, chaos, lazy, lax, unprincipled, easy-going, superficial, unscrupulous, etc. The word conscientiousness is actually an indicator that an individual falling under this category and scoring high on the positive extreme of the domain would have high regard for conscious actions and morality. A strong sense of right and wrong can be present in the person that acts according to his conscience. On the contrary, the person scoring negative on this domain's chart, graph, or the list would tend to exhibit immorality and unprincipled attitude.

✓ The word extraversion technically means to be an extrovert, i.e., easily sociable and interactive. The traits such as talkativeness, sociability, assertiveness, interactivity, gregariousness, outgoingness, friendliness, demonstrativeness, affability, companionability, unreservedness, etc. The lack of extraversion would lead to another extreme involving traits such as shyness, introversion, reservedness, reticence, hesitance, nervousness, isolation, withdrawal, unsociability, self-consciousness, self-efficacy, self-reliance, disinterest, etc.

✓ The term agreeableness is meant to describe characteristics such as tactfulness, warmth, assertiveness, positivity, calmness, attachment, compassion, amiability, nicety, lovability, consideration, kindness, sympathy, and cooperativeness. The opposite of these traits would be harshness, unfeelingness, detachment, indifference, aloofness, remoteness, offensiveness, disagreeableness, uncaringness, repulsiveness, displeasure, negativity, obnoxiousness, etc.

✓ The word Neuroticism is actually derived from the neuroscientific term called neurosis, which means mental impairment or illness that is relatively mild in nature. The derived word neuroticism describes the category of the personality model in the presence of which, people exhibit traits such as nervousness, stress, discomfort, hesitation, turmoil, oversensitiveness, anxiety, anger, jealousy, possessiveness, frustration, fear, guilt, depression, worriedness, moodiness, etc. On the other hand, the lack of neuroticism or a negative range or ranking on the scale of neuroticism may exhibit contrasting traits such as confidence, sense of security and independence, self-content, composure, mental stability, control, collectedness, relaxedness, tranquility, serenity, ease, poise, coolness, etc.

Pioneers of this personality model state that these five domains are so vast and all-inclusive that they encompass all the people out there. Every individual falls under at least one of these categories. Study carefully and understand the person who is to be the subject of your analysis. In which category or under how many categories he may fall and what sort of combinations can be made out of his personality traits after a thorough analysis. Which extremes are apparent in his personality?

CHAPTER 5: WHAT IS MIND READING?

Is mind reading possible? Can humans actually read the emotions and thoughts of a person? Mind reading sounds like a superpower coming straight out of comics. While you cannot communicate with someone miles away from you like Charles Xavier, you can certainly learn this useful skill by gaining knowledge, constant practice, focus, and a certain level of experience. In this chapter, we will discuss some tricks you can learn and apply to read other people's minds. There's something you need to know about mind-reading before you scroll down to learn about these practical tips for getting into someone's head.

Mind Reading - Humans' Inbuilt Feature

Humans are programmed and designed in such a way that it is our second nature to read other people's minds as we interact with them. You might not realize this, but it might have been practiced by you from time to time in your everyday life. The moment you spelled out something and your friend had said at that exact instant, "How do you know I was going to say that?" Just there, you read that person's mind, anticipating the word(s) and uttering it before your friend could say it. This inbuilt ability is present there, and it just needs to be practiced more and more so that it can be polished. Anyone determined enough to polish and sharpen this ability of his cognitive domain should take note of the fact that every human around him has been emitting some sort of an aura or vibes. This may seem such a metaphysical concept, but it is quite true. Your negative or positive feelings may get rub off on someone or vice versa. You can learn to read minds by paying attention to these details. It's just about regaining focus and practicing the following tips:

1. Don't Ignore the Generation Gap

Boomers and Millennials have different values and thinking process. You can learn so much about how a person thinks just by knowing which generation they belong to. Millennials are usually not very social as compared to Boomers. Many Millennials also enjoy jobs which makes them feel independent such as home-based jobs. Boomers, on the other hand, prefer to be on the field and also are more open to face-to-face conversations.

2. Examine Body Language

Body language plays a huge role in reading minds, as will be discussed in upcoming chapters in more detail. Here just note this down as an action step.

Isolate the person from the surroundings imaginatively and focus just on the body of the person. When having a conversation, observe if the person is attentive, does the person looks down, change face direction, or move backward. These are signs that the person is not engaged with you. If someone leans towards you when you speak, it may be interpreted that he is paying attention to what you're saying.

3. Listen Attentively

In a conversation, listen carefully. Having good listening skills can reveal a ton of information about someone's thoughts and emotions. Observe the tone when someone speaks, enthusiasm and frustration are easily recognized. Your welcoming attitude should also encourage others to talk with you as much as possible. The more someone talks, the more they will reveal about themselves.

4. Start a Conservation

A conversation can be a key to someone's thoughts. Asking the right questions is crucial. What does the person value? On what topic you would likely get a strong response? Tell them stories and issues from your own life; more likely than not; they will agree that they have the same or similar issues. This way, you will get a deeper understanding of there problems and their mental state.

5. Personality as a Determinant

As discussed previously, human beings have vastly different personalities. Learning about personalities will make you determine someone's characteristics and what they find significant. An introvert will avoid gatherings and would like to spend time alone rather than hanging out with a group, while an extrovert will prefer to spend time socializing freely.

Mind Reading, Some More Insight:

Mind reading is the art of gaining absolute power within

the cognitive realm of someone. It is not some sort of supernatural magic. Instead, cognitive psychology experts call it a scientific technique involving major cognitive functions such as perception, reasoning, concentration, memorization, and comprehension. It works on the principle of neuroelectric activity taking place in the brain. The electric impulses or neurochemical messages are actually bioelectric signals that make our thoughts, memories, emotions, and feelings a collection of tangible mental structures that are wired systematically in a certain order or manner. The brain works each activity at a different frequency. The subconscious has a relatively lower current or frequency level than the conscious state of mind.

The mind control experts even use a motor car example to describe the microcontroller, i.e., special-purpose computer, characteristics of the brain. At high voltage, the mind generates numerous neuro transmitting impulses that makes the thinking process faster. The mind-reading can also be possible through tangible electronic machines depicting frequencies and impulse wavelengths. The police investigation methods and special screening tests have been invented to use these techniques for reading a person's mind to detect lies, treachery, fear, inhibitions, excitement, and several other emotions and thoughts. What happens is that these detectors or wave readers are attached to a person, scanning his brain, and they can notify when a particular synaptic pathway becomes operational due to the transmission of the neurochemical messages. Numerous researches are still underway to develop this field further.

How to Speed-Read People?

The curiously amazing fact of life is the powerhouse of your entire functioning and actions remain invisible to you. The human mind and the thoughts running in it make up your entire psyche yet; they are often veiled behind the confines of the brain box. The mind-power is interdependent with the other physical forces like experiences, objects, people, etc. The power of a mind to create, think, and analyze wonderfully abundant yet very rarely gets to be used to its full potential.

Speed-reading people is a technique that aims at analyzing people in a quick, definite way according to some pre-decided cues and clues. This is a source of interpretation of both the personality traits and thinking patterns of a person you are analyzing. In the past, reading was limited to books and journals; now, the times have changed. To gain knowledge, traditional reading and studying are not enough. You have to take notice of physical surroundings, observe people, understand their emotions and actions, and learn from life experiences.

The method of speed-reading initially was used to push the brain to deliver its maximum output. The boost to the cognition often results in optimum performance. The person reading an average of 200-250 words per minute is often pushed to perform fast and improve his reading by 600 wpm almost. This is made possible by applying several cues and techniques to the reading method used in order to bring improvement. Now, in the same way, a person observing another individual may overlook many cues if he is a slow or uninterested reader or lacks the necessary skills. If he wants to perform a quick analysis, he must speed up the things.

The speed is gained when you accumulate these skills

while reading people:

✓ *Interest:* You must be interested in your subject, i.e., the person you aim to read.

✓ *Attentiveness:* You must pay attention to minutest details and not miss or overlook anything.

✓ *Confidence:* You must be confident in your observational skills. You must not shy away from glancing around, or look straight into the eyes of the subject in order to read signs, movements, or specific expressions.

✓ *Objectivity:* You must look at the person without prejudice or personal bias in order to gain impartial insight into his personality.

✓ *Concentration:* You must solely be concentrating on the person you are analyzing. Your mind should act as a converging lens, focusing all thoughts on reading that person.

✓ **Clarity of objective:** You must know beforehand why you are speed-reading the person and why you have selected him for this purpose. Make your intentions and goals clear in your mind to speed up the process as confusion slows down the things.

✓ **Dedication:** You must be willing to spend your time speed-reading people. If you cannot dedicate a few minutes of your time observing your subject, do not expect to understand him quickly.

✓ **Order:** You must put your thoughts and acquired insights into an organized pattern to draw sensible, reasonable conclusions. It will be easier to start the reading in a logical sequence such as body language, nonverbal clues, then verbal communication cues, etc.

After making sure these skills are aligned in your goal setting, you can begin to practice speed-reading people with ease and familiarity. The following techniques will let you know the action steps of this process in detail.

TECHNIQUE 7: TRACKING THE COLORS OF THE MIND

This technique explains the thought and personality models in the form of color interpretation, just like color coding works as a memory mnemonic. Experts in this field suggest that the colors have a certain language in which they speak and exhibit their properties. These properties can be possessed by the bearer of that specific color and can have a great deal of influence over his personality and thought process. Even though several practices are already prevalent in this regard. Here we will try to customize this concept a bit to see what conclusions can we draw based on the color tracking technique.

When we set up a model or framework, it means that we are devising a common medium or mechanism for communication of thoughts and actions among the people. The colors of our mind are to be organized in a pattern or mechanism to be interpreted by whoever wants to read into our actions and thoughts. Penetrating deep into the thinking styles makes us aware of the motivations and objectives behind any action of an individual. This technique is a little unique in a way that the colors are universally used and understood yet symbolize different things everywhere. The behavior becomes a function in this technique, while colors are the tools to interpret that function. Experts compare them with ultra-violet rays to detect some "unseen" spectrum of the photograph.

These ultraviolet rays shine on the behavioral patterns and unveil the intricate thoughts behind each one of them. Another important quality of this model is, behaviors and actions become transferrable due to a common, vast medium of colors. The life disciplines such as education, business, marriage, etc. all are interlinked and mutually inclusive. An individual influenced by a specific color and exhibiting a prominent color in one of the disciplines, at some time, may become dominated by shades of other colors that are dominant in other disciplines. This transferability makes a person quite dynamic and flexible in nature which in turn makes him more successful. The working principle of the color mechanism is:

Connecting purposeful thinking to thoughtful action.

The aim of this technique is not just to realize the way a person thinks or attempts to complete a task but to realize the effect of that particular way of thinking on how he attempts to complete that task due to that particular thinking style. This is important so that one can adjust his thinking where it is necessary and develops an improved perception to attempt meaningful task completion. Also, this technique's purpose is not to fixate on a set thinking criteria or notion that you have tracked in yourself or someone else and tailor your actions accordingly but to understand the possible effects of each style and prepare yourself to use any of them per requirement. A sample color chart and mechanism researched by color psychologists, Sue Thame and Jerry Rhodes, is mentioned below for reference.

Follow these actions to understand this technique and implement it:

- Use the color chart or color-coded legend to track

your score by selecting your responses to each action or thought according to your order of preference.

• Understand how people think by matching scores on these charts to know what they think.

• You can customize this chart to provide extended freedom to choose your chosen actions in order to relay the thinking style in a candid, unrestrained manner.

• Be quick and spontaneous in your selection and scoring; don't overthink. The truest response, revealing a person's real thoughts, is the quickest one.

• Don't reveal the color code before the charting in order to get the most accurate and uninfluenced results.

• Note that the score ranges from 0 to 10. In each unit, the maximum score could be 10 for three color-coded action prompts, collectively. For example, if you assign a 0 to the first choice, 3 to the second choice, then the third choice must get a score of 7 to complete the 10 marks quota.

• Know that the three major color domains are Red, Green, and, Blue. All the selected action prompt to track the responses will be falling under these three major color domains.

• The action prompts requiring preferred response

selection will be categorized into units containing a collection of three actions receiving scores according to your preferred level. It will then be added to the score column of each color category to calculate which color domain gets a higher or lower score. (Note: Once you get the hang of it, you can later add more customized units.)

• Color interpretation will be revealed after the charting has been done, and the score has been calculated.

• A simple legend graphic is used as a key to distinguish which action or response belongs to which color category.

Sample Color Scoring Chart with Some Action Prompts

	Score (0-10)
Unit 1	
If you could choose the way to deal with a problem you would prefer to:	
a) Seek out an entirely new solution that surprises others, different from old ways.	......
b) Stick to what seems right and rational.	......
c) Reach a middle ground by opting for what is common and sensible, and what needs improvement.	......
Unit 2	
At the time of event planning, the best thing you like about it is:	
a)Getting to choose between complex yet exciting choices about what should be done.	......
b)Imagining potentially negative outcomes and thinking positive alternatives beforehand.	......
c)Organizing things, sorting them into lists, charts, etc., making preparations.	......
Unit 3	
The best method to shop is:	
a)Keeping my mind open when considering all choices and expecting a newer variety.	......
b)Will be better if I know more about the available product choices before making a choice.	......
c)Will never start until every detail and a list is made to follow systematically.	......

Thinking as a whole is a combination of three component colors; RGB (Red, Green, and Blue). These three aspects or dimensions define the mechanism of your thinking process as a whole, integrated concept. You should add each unit's a's, b's, and c's in separate columns as each action prompt stated in the chart above corresponds to a particular color domain. The added score after calculation should be mentioned in the score section of the table given below relative to the columns of colors that represent a distinctive personality trait or thinking category each. The score legend can be referred to understand the collective score in each category.

Color:	a) Green	b) Red	c) Blue
Score:	. . . . . .	. . . . . .	. . . . . .

Score & Color legend

(Note: The score legend may range from as low as 5 to as high as 70 and above; this will depend entirely on the number of units added in the chart and the number of action prompts' responses being tracked and scored.)

In this scenario, we have three units of action prompts having a total of nine responses. Therefore, our customized sample score legend to determine the dominance of a particular color category or domain will be:

--> **0-5** = You probably avoid thinking in this sort of style. Mostly, this color may get overlooked by you to the point of neglect.

--> **5-10** = You may take this color as an alternative thinking style, i.e., "maybe this as well" sort of thinking.

--> **10-15** = You are able to think more often than not in this color style.

--> **15-20** = You are regularly led by this color domain. Your thoughts are highly motivated by this style.

--> **20 and above** = You tend to overuse this thinking style of color, weakening your potential to use other colors.

The meaning of the colors is the following:

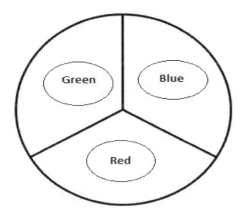

Red says: Describe what is True

Blue says: Judge what is Right

Green says: Realize what is New

Example of how to use this method

Take a pen and paper to write the results I will give you and to understand how to use this methodology.

The example consists of three units, each of the three units proposing three types of answers.

Each answer can be given a numerical score that starts from zero and goes up to 10. The value zero indicates that this action does not belong to you, and you would never do it; the value ten suggests that it is an action that you always do. For each unit, the sum of the scores of the three answers must be 10. For example, if on the answer a) I assigned the score five, to the answer B) I assigned the score three, consequently to the answer c) I will have to assign the score 2.

The meaning of the colors is the following:

Red says: Describe what is True

Blue says: Judge what is Right

Green says: Realize what is New

Now we begin to assign scores to the three units.

UNIT 1

Question: If you could choose to deal with a problem you would prefer to:

Answer a) Seek out entirely new solution that surprises others, different from old ways.

The Score is: 5

Answer b) Stick to what seems right and rational

The score is: 3

Answer c) Reach a middle ground by opting for what is common and sensible, and what needs improvement.

The score is: 2

UNIT 2

Question: At the time of event planning, the best thing you like about it is:

Answer a) How to choose between complex yet exciting choice about what should be done

The Score is: 3

Answer b) Imagining potentially negative features and thinking positive alternatives beforehand.

The score is: 5

Answer c) Organizing things, sorting them into list, charts, etc., making preparations

The score is: 2

UNIT 3

Question: The best method to shop is:

Answer a) Keeping my mind open when considering all choices and expecting a new variety

The Score is: 3

Answer b) Will be better if I know more about the available product choice before making a choice

The score is: 4

<u>Answer c)</u> Will never start until every detail and list is made to follow systematically

The score is: 3

The attribution of the scores of each unit is over. Now all the values of the answers a) of each of the three units must be added together, then all the values of the answers B) of each unit, and finally, all the answers C) of each unit.

The result is the following

Total score answer a): 11

Total score answer b): 12

Total score answer c): 7

The added score after calculation should be mentioned in the score section of the table given below relative to the columns of colors that represent a distinctive personality trait or thinking category each. The score legend can be referred to understand the collective score in each category.

The answer a) represents the color GREEN

The answer b) represents the color RED

The answer c) represents the BLUE color

In this example, we have a prevalence of the answer b), red color, with a score equal to twelve.

This means that you are able to think more often than not in this color style: Judge what is Right.

TECHNIQUE 8: DETECTING TANGIBLE & INTANGIBLE MOOD INFLUENCERS

A person can be categorized by his proactivity or reactivity. According to this technique, we will be discussing ways or signs to detect what ticks a person and how. Unlike the techniques in an initial couple of weeks, here the focus will be more on how rather than on why. People might disagree, but the truth is that the influence can be altered. The objects or emotions, and the thoughts or actions, which influence our mood, can be customized, changed, or blocked out completely on will.

"People are about just as happy as they make up their mind to be." - Lincoln A.

The choices we make determine our daily mood; the more proactive your choices are, the more contented you will feel. The more reactive you become, the more guilt and self-consciousness you will experience. Be a glass of calm water; don't be a bottle of fizzy drink that reacts readily the instance it is stimulated. The analysis of human behavior and personality lets you become more conscious of your own choices as well. While examining the level of proactiveness or reactiveness in your subject, you are likely to self-examine yourself too.

Consider some moods & behaviors as an example:
✓ Putting the blame on someone else is being reactive.
✓ Accepting your shortcomings and still trying to make amends is being proactive.
✓ Holding grudges and making not only others but your own self as well as being reactive.
✓ Forgiving others and your own self as well and adding a new page in life's book in order to move forward is being proactive.

However, not being affected by influencers and blocking them is one thing, while trying to control them is quite another entirely. Some influencers are tangible or physical objects or sensations that affect our state of mind and influence the mood. For e.g. hot weather, rain, rough clothes, cold food, dirty shoes, tangled hair, sweeteners, edible supplements, perfumes, traffic jam, stuffy room, loud noises and commotion, screeching, slapping or physical violence, kisses and hugs, handshakes, pat on the back, sunlight, airy space, warmth inducing material such as a fireplace, etc. Suppose, a person is easily ticked by a display of physical violence. He is sitting with you in a restaurant, talking, and you are observing him, and suddenly you detect a peculiar vibe coming off from his direction, altering his mood. He may seem to be put off by something, suppressing his anger or displeasure. If you are quick to record this mood change, the next step will be to discover how it happened. You look around or follow his direction of the sight to notice a boy being hit by his father in front of the public. You should be able to put two and two together to understand that your subject of analysis may be influenced by this display of violence.

However, if you were not reading this right now, you may have assumed his sudden mood change to be either because of something you did or said or because he just seems like that sort of a moody person who seems to have these unexpected mood swings, so no big deal.

Consider another example. Suppose you are expecting some guests. You have prepared the living room as a reception area. You have cleaned moderately and freshened the air with some sandalwood spray. Your guests come, and you greet and seat them. Upon greeting, you notice one person is not particularly responding. He has a look of distaste on his face and you are startled. You think hard to come up with possible mood-changing agents that could have dampened his mood, and you may realize that it may be due to the unusual fragrance or stuffiness of the room or maybe because of a headache that he has since morning. In all the possible situations, he has been compelled to act in a particular manner, not willingly so. You have to give a person the benefit of the doubt before making faulty assumptions.

Another type of mood influencers is intangible or emotional influencers that include feelings of gratitude, guilt, love, appreciation, nostalgia, etc. Closely related to motivational factors mentioned previously, the major difference between mood influencers and motivational factors is that motivation governs our thoughts and intentions while these thoughts turn into respective actions willingly and intentionally. The mood influencers are mostly the elements that alter our mood or actions unwillingly or unintentionally. While motivation is a need and requirement to perform a particular task, mood influencer is a compulsive agent to affect your train of thoughts, the direction of your response, and the path of your action resulting in often unplanned outcomes. Sometimes, however, people might willingly create an environment possessing desired mood influencers to accelerate the performance and achieve a planned outcome. In this way, the mood influencers act more or less like motivational factors to plan an action. For instance, a person likes to work in a spacious, sunny room with a fragrant atmosphere. He seems to work much better if space is clutter-free and clean. In this situation, he can use the mood influencers positively to enhance his performance. By drawing the curtains, letting the sunlight in, preferring to work in day hours, spraying his favorite scent or using an electric fragrance diffuser in the room, and minimizing the stuff, he may create an environment that lifts up his mood and enhances his work performance. The efforts made to ensure this is also a telling sign of his personality traits such as dedication to work, concentration, hard work, order and organization, and an aversion to mess.

Suppose, your friend may seem to be inattentive and unresponsive to your conversation. You might assume that he is just not interested in what you have to say or complain about. But maybe, at that time, he is more influenced by the huge pile of incomplete work that awaits him at home for which the deadline is nearing. Maybe this is the reason he is preoccupied at the moment, but it does not mean that he doesn't care about you. After all, a huge workload and short deadlines could be a mood dampener for sure. Keeping in mind these possible influencers, practice this technique to understand more about how moodiness shapes an individual's personality.

TECHNIQUE 9: DISCOVERING THE CLIFTON STRENGTHS

Clifton's strengths' concept has been proposed by the

Father Of Strength Psychology, Don Clifton. According to the American Psychological Association (APA), through the invention of these strengths, psychology got a new perspective on the analysis of human personality. Regularly focusing on these strengths and their appearance in a person's personality makes speed-reading them easier and fun. However, a fact must be noted that the mere presence of these strengths may not provide a guarantee for achieving success in life. Research shows that an individual who pays closer attention to his strengths and utilizes them purposefully has higher chances of success and achievement. And those who do not avail of a chance to focus and utilize their strengths are the ones who late regret the lost opportunities in life and remain standing on the same step of the achievement ladder without much progress.

Over the past years, numerous people have attempted the strength-assessment just for the fun of it and without realizing the key purpose behind it. Business models, leadership tests, school exams, career counseling sessions, and psychological therapies, all of them have, in some way or other, make use of this assessment to analyze personalities and behavior models. This assessment can estimate the level of productivity used in both work and relationships. If you make use of these strengths and let others be aware of them as well, you may increase your chances of living in a far more productive environment than what you are experiencing now. You can also understand how Clifton Strengths define distinctive potentials in your personality that can transform in a kinematic manner if motivated appropriately. Another most important feature, apart from motivation, would be to acquire the necessary skills and knowledge about the strength or talent that you think you possess, or a person you are analyzing possesses. This is because, mere talent can get you nowhere if you or any other person possessing it, do not know how to use it properly in a constructive manner.

The working principle of strength psychology is to work and focus more on the already present strengths in a person rather than the absent ones. Because it so happens that we tend to focus more on our shortcomings and the lack or absence of certain strengths in our personalities. Striving to learn them, we tend to forget how to maximize our already present potential and gain expertise in a specific niche area.

As a result, people usually have a superficial knowledge of several things but an in-depth understanding of not even one single area or domain.

Imagine the dilemma of people nowadays. All their lives, they have tried to become what they are not. It is almost like an occupational or psychological hazard. It happens to us as well. Whenever we realize that we have a fault in some areas, and it needs improvement, we automatically start paying more attention to it. This becomes so habitual to us that in our quest to achieve what we are not, or what we lack, we start neglecting what we already have. The ever-present inner qualities bestowed to us, if we take them for granted, they may start working against us instead of working in our favor.

Suppose, your son is quite an enthusiast when it comes to athletic activities. He always performs well in sports. He is, however, quite average when it comes to academics. Whenever you get to see his poor performance report, you realize that he has been lacking in the academics and needs improvement in this area. You motivate him to take remedial classes or enhancement courses, etc. He starts paying more attention to the academics side despite craving for athletic activities. A time comes when he may become above average in academics, but lack of sports practice may transform his excellent performance into a below-average strength or capacity in his much-loved area. An appropriate analysis is needed to understand which strengths are present in a person and why they should be retained and polished even more.

Research has shown that although we, humans, are creatures possessing adaptability, some traits remain stable, lying there, in our personality core. They are not much affected by time, mood change, or other influential factors such as our passions, interests, talents, etc. Clifton Strength finder attempts to assess these sorts of more stable strengths present in the people.

Experts suggest that people who start with raw talent and follow it with necessary investment, knowledge, skills, professional training and expertise actually multiply their chances of success and productivity, effectively reducing the chances of time wastage and extra hard work, overly struggling to achieve little or no return. Therefore, sooner than later, people must discover their strengths and team them up with all the right elements to make a perfect recipe for strength and success. As an analyzer of people and their personality, you must realize the ground fact that,

---

"Every individual has talents and strengths, just waiting to be unearthed from the garden soil of their personality." -- I F.

The strength finding assessment does not aim to supply people with strengths they want to acquire, but help in locating your areas of potential talents and latent strengths or abilities. The following are the famous 34 Clifton strengths found in people. These strengths are listed in alphabetic order:

1. Achiever: A constant inner drive to achieve. This strength motivates you to have an achievement every day, however small it may seem, in order to feel a sense of accomplishment and satisfaction.

2. Activator: A person has this strength if he is

constantly looking for some action and active participation in a task. You would have often heard some team members of a project asking, "When can the work be started?" or "Shall we go ahead then?". Once a task has been planned, they carve for some prompt action.

3. Adaptability: This one is a present-day man. Always adjusting and living in the moment. He is able to respond willingly and adapt according to the situational demands despite having made prior plans.

4. Analytical: This person is constantly presenting others with challenging concepts to prove, show, exemplify, etc., the facts and scenarios. This person is quite objective and not easily swayed by emotions. He remains steadfast in his opinions and continues searching for ground realities to understand the possible relationship between facts and judgments.

5. Arranger: This means an individual is able to conduct and manage several simple and complex things in an organized manner and enjoys finding the best way to do so.

6. Belief: This person has a strong sense of altruism, righteousness, a general love for spirituality, strong moral conduct, and a fixed belief system that has enduring values which he follows in every walk of life.

7. Command: It makes a person take charge and control other people and situations. The person possessing this strength often imposes his views and commands others. He has a confident persona and doesn't hesitate to confront and take risks.

8. Communication: This person loves to speak, write, host, and present. He likes to be in contact with the public in one way or another. He is often seen narrating past memories, stories, and life incidents in social gatherings to extend people's attention span and divert it towards him.

9. Competition: This person's sense of achievement is always dependent on the rate of other people's success. He is compelled to compare and outperform his peers to feel more successful. He thrives for the challenging win and the

excitement that comes with it.

10. Connectedness: This individual sees the world as an integrated sphere. Each person is linked to another; every action relates to a cause or motive. This person knows about how closely linked humans living in a society are and the mutual responsibilities that come with this connection.

11. Consistency: This means believing in quality and regularity over quantity and sporadicity. Balance is this person's principle. He tends to maintain fairness in every relation and work objective.

12. Context: This person lives in the present by relating it to the past. He uses his prerequisite knowledge of past experiences to understand present questions and situations.

13. Deliberative: Vigilance, carefulness, privacy, cautiousness, and a reserved attitude just about sums up this strength.

14. Developer: This person is always looking for hidden

potentials and talents in other people. He is someone who enjoys facilitating further development of these potentials by his speech, actions, and guidance. He takes each human being as a work in progress, exploring and thriving on possible chances of further growth and improvement.

15. Discipline: He is a predictable individual needing an orderly life. He needs everything to be planned ahead of time in order to avoid physical disturbance or mental chaos.

16. Empathy: This person has an inbuilt radar to sense the emotions and feelings of those around him.

17. Focus: The one driven by this talent needs a clear goal to strive for. He needs to set his priorities straight to help him focus on which path should be taken in life to achieve his goal.

18. Futuristic: This person likes to look ahead in the direction of the future, trying to foresee his life after the present has become the past.

19. Harmony: Harmony means the person believes in the goodness of a conflict-free environment. He is quite agreeable. He likes to settle an arising conflict by reach mutual agreement and maintaining a harmonized environment.

20. Ideation: This one is a brainstormer, an innovator, and an idea generator. He is readily fascinated by ideas and their connections to things, tasks, and people.

21. Includer: "Make room for others too." The person working by this philosophy is likely to be an Includer. He is accepting a person, welcoming as many people in his circle as possible to not make them feel left out. He believes in equal opportunities.

22. Individualization: More or less an antonym for inclusiveness, the person having this strength tends to detect the individual qualities of the people. He does not like to generalize people, hates stereotypes, and generic groups that overshadow the individual potential of a person.

23. Input: This person likes to investigate and search for answers. He likes to gather information, interesting things like coins, books, pictures, etc. Each action is done to have an input, i.e., knowledge and a new perspective on something, someplace, or some person. This individual is curious about the world, as though he was the computer seeking input from peripheral devices such as sensory organs and environmental factors, etc.

24. Intellection: An intellectual likes to think and function through cognitive activities that exercise the brain.

25. Learner: This person is a seeker of knowledge. He derives excitement and thrill from the process of gaining knowledge and the prospect of being able to comprehend things.

26. Maximizer: He is a perfectionist. An excellence-seeker. He does not care for below average results. He targets optimum performance.

27. Positivity: This person is optimistic and generous. He

is looking at the pros rather than the cons in a given situation.

28. Realtor: This person has a close-knit circle of friends and family in whose company he feels contented. He may not exhibit shyness in meeting new people, he might even enjoy it sometimes due to certain reasons, but he still prefers to be closer to his loved ones and be in familiar company.

29. Responsibility: The responsible person always takes ownership of his commitments and duties. He feels morally and emotionally obliged on his own accord, to fulfill his promises and roles honorably. He has a sense of integrity and feels bound to compensate if, in case, he could not deliver on a promise.

30. Restorative: This person thrives to restore the damages that have been done. He takes on challenging problems and comes up with solutions. While other people make mistakes and run away from making up for them or correcting them. He sets the problem straight and puts the situation right by seeking the root cause of trouble, conceptualizing the solution, and implementing it.

31. Self-Assurance: This person has faith in his abilities. He has a "can-do" attitude. This means that an individual not only has confidence in his potential strengths but also in his judgment.

32. Significance: This person strives to be recognized for his abilities and hard work. Given significant importance to his abilities makes him feeling more energized and appreciated. He likes to stand out from the crowd in a noticeable stance.

33. Strategic: Sorting through the various themes and choices, and reaching the best method to implement, is what strategic person does.

34. Woo: This one is a public pleaser. People are easily won over by him due to his likable personality, whether they are strangers or not.

CHAPTER 6: COMMUNICATION AND PERSONALITY

Communication is the process of sharing. It has derived from the Latin word "communico." When two or more persons meet, they share information, feelings, ideas, thoughts, etc. Communication is a continuous process of speaking listening and understanding. Communication is a skill. Most people are born with the physical ability to talk, but to speak well and coherently, one must have to adapt certain key characteristics to make his communication skills perfect. Good communication skills build your personality. It gives you confidence and boosts your self-esteem thus giving your personality a sober and sophisticated look.

Communication is the most vital means by which people are connected in society, and a lack of good communicational skills can make society a miserable place to live. So, for living in a peaceful environment, its necessary that man should have good communication skills. Today, the most successful person is the one who can communicate effectively. Good communication build strong personalities, and strong personalities make great decisions. It's the skill a man develops until the day he dies. There is no limit to developing and improving this specific skill. Humans must keep moving and trying to improve their personalities further with proper communication techniques. Remember, we are here judging their methods to communicate rather than their skills in effective communication. You would be analyzing people this week by the way they communicate.

Nonverbal Communication

Another important element of communication is non-verbal communication. Nonverbal communication is interpersonal communication with linguistic means. The non-verbal message conveys feelings more accurately than those of verbal means. The non-verbal communication process comprises of several factors like appearance, facial expressions, eye contact, gestures, touch, postures, voice, space, and time. Nonverbal communication is everything except words. When it comes to appearance, your personality speaks itself. A person's personality appearance can affect the impressions others receive of his credibility, honesty, competence, judgment, or status.

A person's face is more capable of communicating nonverbally than other parts of the human body. The face sends messages about his emotions like happiness, sorrow, frustration, fear, etc. In fact, we don't have to ask people about their feelings. Their facial expressions reveal their present emotional state. Similarly, when it comes to effective nonverbal communication, eye contact is the main factor in reflecting one's intention through his eye movements. Direct eye contact shows the confidence level, whereas the breaking of eye contact gives the signals of shyness to other people.

You can predict a person's intentions just by the gestures he is showing. For example, nail-biting shows the nervousness of a person, nodding head shows agreement, and a thumbs-up signal is used to show appreciation. This is how people communicate with gestures without even saying a single word. Though the communication is nonverbal, the exclamatory sounds coming from a person's mouth can transfer the message he wants to deliver. For instance, if he has gotten hurt accidentally, an "ouch" sound comes from his mouth, which shows his pain or discomfort. Likewise, if he is in a sorrowful mood or feeling melancholic, he sighs, which communicates his sad emotions.

These factors make nonverbal communication strong and powerful. One cannot deny the role of gestures, eye contact, facial expressions, and other similar cues that help in effective nonverbal communication. It is a built-in natural instinct in living beings to communicate. When language was not there, still people managed to communicate with each other through different body gestures and postures or even graphical symbols. Effective communication is important whether it is verbal or nonverbal, and the intentions are a vital part of all the means of communication. During your analysis, when you observe the person communicating something verbally or nonverbally, you must look for possible answers to the questionable intentions of your subject.

Week 3

TECHNIQUE 10: SPOT THE BODY LANGUAGE (GESTURES, STANCE, POSTURE, ETC.)

This one is the most important aspect of nonverbal communication and is relatively easier to detect. When a person stops speaking, the body starts communicating. The focus of the audience is directed towards each hand gesture that is portrayed, and each posture that the body represents. The stance is also important to notice in people who are mostly moving about or standing nearby, such as in the queues or at restaurant counters, etc. The following are four body postures that may be attributed to certain personality traits.

• A person standing with a straight back. This is a neutral posture depicting a calm, assured manner of behavior.

• A person maintaining leaning forward in a collapsing posture. It reveals the giving up attitude or depressed mood of a person.

• A person maintaining an upright position with spread

arms and feet wide apart. This often exhibits a confident, open-minded attitude with a dominant stance.

• A person slightly inclining toward the other person while standing beside him. This represents a sweetly sympathetic gesture. For example, a teacher leans towards his student while listening to him.

While analyzing a personality, it must be noted that the interpretation of these gestures or postures is still quite subjective in nature despite being researched time and again. This is because humans often display unpredictable, sudden responses, yet in the long run, these patterns may become predictably repetitive due to observation and consistent analysis. Therefore, once you start practicing, you will begin to predict the expected responses of your subject or even guess their alternatives in a given situation.

TECHNIQUE 11: PERCEIVE THE EYE MOVEMENT

They say that eyes are sort of windows to the human soul. How much correct depends on the keenness of the beholder during his observation. Each glance matters, and each movement is recorded by the serious individual dedicated to learning this technique of analyzing people. There can be definite relativity between eye movement and cognitive activity as described by the famous psychologist William James.

Consider these points when observing eye movements:

1. Pupil dilation usually means attraction and interest in the percieved person.
2. There are 6 specific eye movements in the generalized version of the theory. VR, VC, AR, AC, AD, and K.
    o VR (Visually remembered): Directed to the upper left
        ▪ remembering images previously seen
    o VC (Visually constructive): Directed to the left side
        ▪ creating images haven't seen before
    o AR (Auditively remembered): Directed to the lower left
        ▪ remembering images previously heard

o AC (Auditively constructive): Directed to the upper right

- creating sounds or voices that haven't been heard before by you. For e.g. , upcoming viva questions by the examiner.

o AD (Digitally Auditive): Directed to the right side

- focusing on the voice of internal dialogue

o K (Kineasthetic): Directed to the lower right

- the eyes are focusing on sensory perception, bodily sensations, and experiencing emotions such as the feel of ice melting on the hand.

-

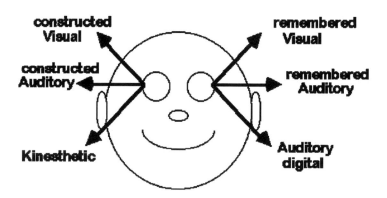

TECHNIQUE 12: READ THE FACIAL EXPRESSIONS

The face holds the main emotions and expressions of a person. Being the center of attraction and observation, it can convey numerous meaningful signs to communicate a particular message. If verbal communication is not paired with appropriate facial expressions, the words become quite meaningless. On the other hand, even if the person remains silent, the facial expression or his gestures can say it all. That is why the pantomime has become such an effective presentation method. The facial expressions are the responses stimulated by mood, thoughts, and the surrounding environment of a person. If he is angry due to disturbing noise, his face will portray his displeasure, and if he is listening to a melancholic sound of a prayer, his expression may become wistful. The strong facial expressions may carry a kind of power in them, intimidating others or letting them become apprehensive such as looking into an interviewer's confidently strong face may confuse a job applicant for a while.

You will have to learn this technique to ensure you know what their faces show!

TECHNIQUE 13: CHECK THE HANDWRITING AND DOODLING

The handwriting of a person is a strong indicator of his state of mind. For a great observer, keen on subtle signs that reflect an individual's personality, pen or pencil strokes on the surface of a paper becomes a medium of silent communication. These strokes and marks define how a person is feeling. Lazy doodling appearing almost as an illegible script symbolizes the instability of emotions. Whereas, strong strokes with a purposeful grip on the pencil tells us about the clear-headed state of the writer's mind.

Too much pressure exerted on the writing tool while writing may also reveal the passionate nature of the person. There is a whole new branch of psychological sciences called Graphology which deals with the personality analysis of individuals by judging their handwriting. US National Pen Company states that there may be more than 5000 personality traits revealed just by interpreting the dynamics of a person's handwriting style. Factors such as spacing, letter-size, the particular shape of individual letters, pen pressure, etc. are determinants in this regard.

TECHNIQUE 14: CHECK THE PREFERRED COLOR OF CLOTHES

The colors are also powerful mood influencers and personality indicators. The famous profiling system called true colors is based on their effects on the person's strengths and shortcomings and their further enhancement. For instance, the green personality type is often more loyal than others, while the orange one is less passionate and calmer than the red one. Wearing these colors according to the order of preference describes the nature of that individual and matching his actions with the prescribed color traits might describe the reason for his choice in the long run.

TECHNIQUE 15: NOTICE THE SILENCE AND SMILE

They say silence is more powerful than speech. Once a

person becomes silent, his inner personality starts emitting vibes that attract the focus of a person keenly observing him. It is like the soul of a silent person is calling people to come read its feelings and emotions. Some people prefer to remain silent throughout the conversation and only smile at appropriate times to denote a required response. This means that they prefer to actively listen and comprehend your words, instead of interrupting you. It also can mean that these people are wiser than most people because they measure their words well and cherish them. You would see that when eventually they decide to speak, their concise words contain a wealth Of sensible advice and actionable wisdom which they learned through silently listening and contemplating.

TECHNIQUE 16: RECORD THE RESPONSES TO CERTAIN STIMULI

The environment is your stimulator. It contains sensory diodes to trigger the thought process. A study conducted in the past suggested a technique called DTR, i.e., Disrupt than refrain to stimulate people by showing them tantalizing call-to-action scenarios or procedures. You can follow this technique by noticing how people get influenced by words or actions if arrange in a peculiarly different manner or sequence.

For, e.g., some people might believe $299 to be way cheaper than $300 at first glance. This is called confusing the waters or playing with the psyche. Similarly, notice how people often react when told about time in terms of minutes instead of hours. It makes their brain perplexed while processing the concept of time in less frequent terms, and therefore, helps the simulator to achieve the desired response. Observe the stimuli projected in front of people and record their way of reactions in this sort of situation. Another sort of active stimulus in the surroundings to trigger the desired response in people would be to hang a large pair of eyes in a public area such as a park or restaurant, for instance. This will make people have a psychological response in their conscience. They will be more careful to follow the rules of that particular place like avoid littering the place, etc.

CHAPTER 7: VERBAL COMMUNICATION

No communication is completed until the message is received by the receiver. And to make sure that the message has been reached to the specific person properly, people strive to find better ways to reach their audience as the message must have to be communicated in a proper manner. In communication, a principle of sharing is evident. But this sharing needs appropriate verbal communication techniques. A person's personality gets doomed when they open their mouths, and insignificant words come out. It needs proper work and time to enhance and improve an individual's verbal communication skills. No one is born perfect. But people work hard to achieve perfection. Experts believe that good verbal skills are important for your carrier, relationships, and self-esteem.

Verbal communication plays a powerful role in the enhancement of one's personality, career development, and happy personal life. We all are bound directly or indirectly with each other as we move along together in a society. We need to communicate at every step of our lives. We need words to define emotions, thoughts, objects, and behaviors. But these are not just words; these are the verbal skills we learn by the passage of time and with people from whom we interact. Similarly, the person you are going to analyze will also be communicating using more or less the same skills and methods for the same goals and purposes. Thus, understanding them becomes easier.

Pretext Communication

Pretext communication is dodging another person in a manner that he realizes the real reason for some specific act later. It is about misinterpreting or hiding information. For example, Anna called her friend on a sleepover without giving her a hint that she wants to complete her homework with her.

Contextual communication

It is the form of communication in which both parties know about the exchange of information on account of cultural, environmental, and relational contexts. To explain it better, consider an example of Bluetooth or mobile verification process. When we use mobiles, we have to go through biometrics or personal information sharing, and both sides know the input and output of the shared information. This is called contextual communication.

Sub-textual Communication

The subtext is an underlying emotion or intention. It lies behind the actual communication acting like an unspoken dialogue amidst the spoken words. As communication experts say that a person's voice is a vehicle carrying several passengers such as emotions, intonations, and pretexts, and subtexts. Suppose, you are hearing a person delivering a speech about flood victims in a charity fundraiser. You hear him speak seemingly practical words, but his voice carries an underlying sympathy and care for the cause. This behind the curtain's emotion is a sub-textual part of an otherwise ordinary conversation. Similarly, you often find yourself saying "Don't worry, I am fine" with an angry tone, to a nagging friend who keeps on asking if you are okay. When in reality, your voice suggests your anger and sadness and defies your actual words. The art of analyzing people through their communication styles makes you quickly realize these underlying intonations and understand the real intention of a person regardless of what his words are. You may have heard, actions speak louder than words, but here actually, the tone is far more revealing than the word itself.

Intertextual Communication

Even though, according to popular opinion, intertextuality means the explanation of one text in terms of another text or exploring the interrelationship of similar textual pieces. Here, in terms of communication, intertext means to relate the saying or communicative expression of a person to another one that he or she or some other person said or expressed. This way, a person's thoughts, and uttered expressions can be defined and explained through references in a relative manner. The metaphors, quotations, or allusions are sometimes used as intertextual devices. People often communicate in an intertextual manner when they attempt to cite another author or person's sayings to relate to their opinions or statements.

The role of verbal skills is very significant and important

as we cannot stay mute for hours. We need to share. We need to communicate; we need to interact for the reason of survival. Man cannot survive without letting out the thoughts, feelings, and emotions. And this can only be possible with coherent and concise verbal communications. There are some barriers also which affect verbal communication such as distractions, lack of interest, emotional barriers, the difference in point of view, physical disabilities like hearing problems, speech difficulties, etc. These can be the cause of ineffective verbal communication. The most important barrier is the linguistic barrier as will be discussed below.

Types of Communication Barriers

As mentioned earlier, interpersonal communication may fail because of different communication barriers. An emotionally intelligent person strives to learn empathy by overcoming barriers in communication. This individual tries to learn methods of effective communication by analyzing another person's way of communication; therefore, he must understand that sometimes, these barriers are unavoidable. Obstacles such as distortion or disturbance during a conversation, a disturbed state of mind, or moodiness may become the cause of miscommunication among individuals. Due to these factors, the chances of misunderstandings increase exponentially during communication, and this results in a lack of successful comprehension of the transmitted message.

Communication barriers may vary in nature. Some of them are psychological, linguistic, physical, cultural, emotional, etc. See the details of these barriers below:

1. Linguistic Barriers

The main one is the language barrier that can affect effective communication. Language is an essential communication tool. Every state has its specific language and a thick dialect. If you are unaware of the language or dialect of a region, it can make communication nearly impossible in some cases. Nor can a person being unaware of the language of another individual be able to analyze his voice intonation or verbal expressions.

2. Psychological Barriers

Several psychological and mental issues can disturb

effective communication. These issues may vary in people, such as speech disorders, stage fear, depression, phobia, etc. Sometimes, it can be challenging to manage these conditions.

3. Emotional Barriers

Your emotional IQ determines the comfort and ease of communication. An emotionally mature person can communicate effectively. For effective communication, you will need a perfect blend of facts and emotions. Particular emotions like humor, sadness, fear, frustration, and anger may blur your executive capacities.

4. Physical Barriers

Physical barriers are represented by closed doors or cabins, noise, faulty equipment (used for communication), etc. You can remove these barriers easily by using alternatives to facilitate effective communication. Sometimes, physical separation between numerous employees and dependency on some defective equipment for communication can decrease the effectiveness of the mutual interface.

5. Cultural Barriers

The world is becoming globalized; therefore, a large office often contains people from different regions of the world. Remember, the meaning of a word can be different in every culture. Drinks, food, pets, and general behavior may vary drastically in each culture.

For effective communication, you have to consider different cultures during a conversation. Companies may offer specialized courses at their orientation stages. The purpose of these courses is to teach tolerance and courtesy to people from different cultures. In order to be efficient in reading people's behavior and approaching them with the right attitude without causing an offense intentionally or unintentionally, you have to identify and address these communication barriers appropriately.

TECHNIQUE 17: NOTE THE GREETING & FAREWELL

The conversation your subject is having will have an opening and an end. This technique lets you focus on the way he opens the conversation with people by greeting them and the way he closes it by saying his farewell. You would have to focus on his style of greeting his guests, host, or appointed help in the office environment.

- Note, does he say "Hi, what's up!" or "Hey/Hello" in a conversational, candid manner or "Good Evening / Good day to you, etc." in a stiff tone? The former will let you know his informal and friendly personality while the latter may suggest a bit more formal and reserved attitude. The excitement, pent up anticipation, and overwhelming joy can also be conveyed through the warmth of the greeting, whereas the suppressed annoyance or displeasure on seeing someone unexpected or unwelcomed can be revealed through the cold, distant greeting message.

- Similarly, notice how he quotes his farewell message. A person who is quite reluctant to leave someone's precious company will often be regretful while saying his farewell. His words would portray his eagerness to meet again, such as "Can't wait to see you again soon." While a person finding another's company boring or offensive will be impatient to take his leave. His parting words may reveal how glad he is to finally have the chance to escape such as "I think I should go now as I have something quite important to attend to, excuse me."

TECHNIQUE 18: NOTE THE CONVERSATION IN BETWEEN

The research shows how often people tend to overwhelm their audience by wordy phrases and nonstop banter. It sometimes shows that with an unfavorable audience, people fill their conversational address with continuous verbal messages that are complicated to be processed quickly by the brain. This way, the chances of any disapproval are lessened, and an expected argument can be avoided. Diverting the conversation to a person's favorite topic can also grab his interest. A person showing extra quietness or responding with hmms and aahs can also be deemed uninterested or preoccupied.

TECHNIQUE 19: READ BETWEEN THE LINES (UNDERSTAND THE INNUENDOS)

The popular "Inneundo Effect" suggests that people can be saying something positive and another, less positive thing can be inferred from their words. The fact is that you must learn this technique if you want to understand what people say and what they really think or intend to do. An open mind and an observing eye can notice numerous things. Try to read between the lines as merely visible text interpretation might not be enough while analyzing people and speed-reading their minds.

While your subject may seem quite disinterested in buying a particular book, he may be fixated on some alternative approach such as listening to a program on the same topic instead. He may say, "Interesting topic it is, but I am not buying that book, you do that. I am not that much into reading complex books. I prefer spending my time listening to radio programs."

Even if he has not clearly declared that he wants to know

more about the topic, he has expressed that he thinks it to be interesting. He has also stated that he is more into listening to the radio than reading complex books. But he hasn't declared the topic to be complex, just the format of its presentation. This means that he may be finding alternative ways to search and know more about the topic that he too has found interesting. Thus, as a person analyzing him, you may understand him more if you read between the lines of this conversation, not just the words that have clearly been said, but also the words that were just insinuated or implied.

TECHNIQUE 20: UNDERSTAND THE LANGUAGE AND SPEECH DEVICES

This technique focuses on learning the language of the person you are analyzing and the popular literary devices used in that particular language. Metaphors, similes, analogies, allusions, anagrams, amplification, anecdotes, anthropomorphism, allegory, euphemism, etc.

TECHNIQUE 21: LEARN TO DIFFERENTIATE BETWEEN HUMOR, SATIRE, AND PUN, ETC.

Sometimes, due to lack of awareness and skills, a joke is often taken too seriously, or a serious statement is often judged as bad humor. This can become a hindrance to the understanding of the general public. To learn this technique, you will have to study the difference between humor, satire, and pun, etc.

Humor: Anything that can provoke a laughing response or stimulate a smile.

Satire: Anything that is used to express irony, ridicule, scorn, or mockery of a particular concept or belief. It uses humor and exaggeration as one of the methods.

Pun: Intended for amusement purpose, it is a figure of speech. Used as a wordplay to induce multiple meanings or using homophones in a rhetorical or humorous sense.

TECHNIQUE 22: NOTICE THE EMPHASIS ON CERTAIN SPOKEN WORDS BY THE SPEAKER

The stress on certain words can reveal their importance in the voice of the communicator.

- Listen carefully.
- Notice the way the speaker is uttering or articulating each word.
- Notice his facial expression and concentration while he emphasizes on particular words or syllables of a word.

TECHNIQUE 23: NOTICE THE EMOTIONS AND WAY OF DIALOGUE DELIVERY MORE THAN THE WORDS

The expressions convey way more emotions than unfeeling words. You may consider a person cold because of his distant or reserved personality, but before you make an opinion about him, you must;

- Look into the expressions and feel the undercurrent's

emotions and feelings of a person rather than just paying attention to his dialogue.

• Instead of just hearing what he delivers, see how he delivers it.

• Notice how his throat may clog up while speaking brief, courteous words, due to the depth of his emotions.

TECHNIQUE 24: OBSERVE HOW THE SPEAKER IS RESPONDING TO CRITICISM, DISAGREEMENT, AND CONFRONTING STATEMENTS WHILE BEING ENGAGED IN A CONVERSATION

Through practicing this technique, an important aspect of your subject can be revealed. In the face of disapproval and while being confronted with disagreement, people often lose their cool.

• A person ready to accept his mistakes and reflect on them in order to improve himself will confront the disagreement in an agreeable manner.

• While a person thinking himself to be always right can be stubborn and never comfortable or cool while responding to even constructive criticism, he will try to start the blame game instead.

TECHNIQUE 25: OBSERVE HOW AN INDIVIDUAL IS RESPONDING TO APPLAUSE AND COMPLIMENTS

This technique involves noticing an individual at the time of receiving compliments and being praised. The one who is full of himself, showing signs of narcissism, may accept this praise as his birthright and take it for granted. However, the one having a modest behavior, moderate thoughts, and a grateful personality takes each compliment as a motivation to work harder and improve himself further. The one who does not lose his mind over constant applause and remains focused on his goals is the truly successful person. You would see how people get swayed by praise and forget how to be thankful. For e.g., team leaders often take all the credit for the success of a project forgetting to include their team members who have huge behind-the-scene efforts and hard work to their credit.

CHAPTER 8: ART OF PERSUASION AND INFLUENCING PEOPLE

You often have heard people making complaints about the communication gap or their inability to convince people effectively. Remember, your ability to influence and persuade people to get the things as per your desire depends upon your way of addressing them and your overall persona. In order to be better capable of making the environment to sing to your tune and people to walk your talk, you have to learn the ways to persuade people, to earn their respect, and get the support of your customers, coworkers, bosses, friends, and colleagues, etc.

Numerous people don't know that human communication involves a complicated process of influence and persuasion. For this reason, they are the ones being often persuaded to assist others instead of influencing people to support them. Personal will power and inner strengths can make you a persuasion expert. With your personal powers of confidence, self-belief, steadfastness, and a strong tone of voice, you can get your message across to your audience. You would have often seen how public speakers strategize their speeches and describe actionable pieces of advice to motivate their listeners. You can analyze that most of them derive these meaningful bits of advice and suggestions from their life experiences. They describe real-life examples to reach the masses and get them to relate easily to what they are saying.

Week 5

Motivation is key to persuasion. Each human action needs some motivation. If you want to analyze how a strong motivational speaker successfully influences his audience and convinces them, make sure to find out whether he is addressing them through mood influencers or motivational factors. People can be motivated by fear of failure and desire for profit. Make sure to work on these motivational factors to get desired results. The speakers often address these issues by stating relatable examples so that people actually feel compelled to respond to the call of action. There is also a famous mirror effect that depicts how people tend to subtly imitate other people in their way of speaking, and body gestures, etc. to project a feeling of familiarity and get their approval. Below are the actionable steps to summarize how to understand the art of influencing people through motivation and persuasion.

TECHNIQUE 26: LISTEN TO PUBLIC MOTIVATIONAL SPEAKERS

The best way of getting inspiration is by listening to

motivational speeches.

✓ Pay attention to the actions, communication style, and body language of motivational speakers. These people can help you to develop your own communication style.

✓ Listen to the motivational speakers telling about real-life anecdotes combined with wisdom and experience.

✓ See how they interact with a group of people to stimulate their desire to achieve personal goals. With positive advice and anecdotes, it will be easy for you to analyze how people deal with pitfalls and failures of life.

TECHNIQUE 27: NOTICE PERSUASIVE STYLES IN MONOLOGUE AND DIALOGUE

Dialogue and monologue are literary devices in speeches. Monologue means the delivery of a speech by a character to express his feelings and thoughts to other characters. Dialogues are conversations between different characters. Remember, monologue refers to a lecture or speech delivered by one person only. Dialogue means a conversation between 2 to 3 or even more people. For instance, a TV show, talk show, or influential forum, etc.

You can reveal your inner character through monologue. If you want to address a crowd, you have to work on your monologue. For a conversation between 2 or more characters, it is essential to improve your dialogue. Remember, dialogue may portray the interaction style of a character. You can reveal your ideas and thoughts through dialogues. You will need an energetic style for your dialogue and monologue.

If you want to become an influential speaker, you have to work on your monologue and dialogue. It can be done through motivational speeches and talk shows. Listen to their speaking style and practice these skills in front of others. You can't become an influential executive without persuasive dialogue and monologue. To become a perfect speaker, start practicing in front of your friends and family members.

TECHNIQUE 28: OBSERVE THE WAY PEOPLE DEAL WITH THEIR SUBORDINATES

Active dealing with people is necessary for your workplace. With persuasive communication skills, dealing with workers and colleagues can be both a challenge and a joy. You must have the ability to deal with people in the workplace. For this reason, observe other employers and notice their way to deal with their subordinates.

It is essential to demonstrate a certain level of respect and consideration for people in the workplace or social circles. Along with respect, trust is a cornerstone when communicating with people. Faith becomes the foundation of positive communication, employee motivation, and interpersonal skill. To become an influential speaker, you have to practice active listening skills.

Do you want to get feedback from other people about your work? Make it easy with your body language and behavior. If you're going to become a persuasive speaker or analyze one who already is, feedback is necessary for both. Feedback permits you to adjust your style in dealing with people, challenges, and situations at work.

As a boss, you are responsible for communicating with your employees, coworkers, and colleagues. With your communication skills and gesture, you must tell them that you value their contribution to your business. It is a powerful way to influence people to follow your directions. They will be ready to work in your favor.

TECHNIQUE 29: OBSERVE THE WAY THEY RESPOND TO THEIR BOSS

For successful business operations, cooperate communication is a crucial element. Interacting with top-level management can be a real challenge. If you want to become an influential speaker, you have to notice the response of motivational speakers to their bosses. People often get intimidated by their employers upon meeting them. This often happens with new employees.

Boss and employees should be in a certain comfort zone; for this reason, they have to spend time to get familiar with each other. This may happen through short appraisal meetings, interviews, etc. A middle manager can interact with juniors more frequently and pass on the essential employee details to the boss. Some people to stay in touch with their bosses through middle management. Some people regard communication with their boss mildly challenging yet compete for it too, like a game of friendly chess. They feel compelled to stay ahead of their colleagues.

Consider yourself to be the person you are analyzing. How would you behave around your boss? A good employee always anticipates the needs of his/her boss. As an employee, paying attention to the working style and habits of your boss is important too. This helps improve your communication skills and job performance. You must have the ability to identify potential problems and offer possible solutions.

Notice the personality style and approach of both the boss and his employee. Their work relationship will help you understand their behavior model. If the boss likes to communicate over the phone instead of email, Employees often adjust and fine-tune their verbal communication skills. Some employees strictly follow the rule of sticking to business. They feel that there is no need to become friendly with their boss, indulging in personal conversations. Instead, their seriousness to work directs them to believe that the job needs a genuine interest in all things professional in contrast to personal bonding.

TECHNIQUE 30: OBSERVE THE WAY THEY COMMUNICATE AND WORK WITH THEIR PEERS AND FAMILY

✓ Focus on others when they talk and work with their peers and family. Excellent communication skills are always required to create successful relationships with peers and family. Active listening is necessary to understand others and tell them that you always value their feedback.

✓ Observe. Do people pay attention to others' opinions and statements? How much they care and value their thoughts?

✓ Observe. Are they more comfortable in a familiar company than they were in the work environment or more professional climate?

✓ Observe and analyze your findings and match the results with the personality models to understand which category a person may belong to.

✓ Some people do follow effective techniques of communication. They make eye contact, move, or turn toward their conversation partner and a nod to their ideas. They try to ignore all possible distractions to increase their focus on their partner. These people are considered good listeners and considerate confidants among their peers and family.

Paying attention to the feelings and content behind each spoken word, they try to understand where their friends are coming from. Some people even exhibit the ability to understand emotions like anger, excitement, sadness, and joy through people's body language. This shows their keenness and excellent observational skills as well as their interest in others. A person full of himself, always talking, and making others listen may not be able to spare the chance of noticing these delicate nuances that define people and their personalities. Don't be that sort of a person and practice the art of becoming emotionally intelligent.

CHAPTER 9: CONFLICT RESOLUTION AND HUMAN BEHAVIOR

The conflict resolution is an important and integral requirement within different aspects of real life. The human-specific behavior, in connection with the conflict-oriented situations and the specific response to them, is based on experience as well as the understanding of individuals in connection with conflicts. There is a possibility of different conflicts you come across the life of the individuals. The conflicting situations can usually arise when one person or group would start to emphasize on the fact that its interests are undermined. The nature and the complexity of the conflict can depend upon the understanding level as well as the human-specific behavior responding to that particular conflict-oriented environment.

A better understanding of the environment, as well as an exploration of different possibilities to resolve a particular problem and the conflict, can be productive for the people and the organizations. This helps them manage conflicting situations in a better way.

The human-specific behavior, in response to a particular conflict, has to be focused on the fact to understand the conflict in the first place. It is important for individuals and human beings getting into a conflicting situation to give the maximum level of the time for developing a better understanding of the different stances and points of view related to the conflict. The mutually agreeable place and time discuss the details of the conflict-oriented situation with respect to developing a better understanding of its dynamics and can play a positive and constructive role in its resolution. Each of the individual companies in the conflict-oriented situation has to come out to express its understanding as well as point of view about the conflict-oriented situation. It becomes significantly important for human beings to try to focus on the development of a better understanding of ideas and thinking of other people who are involved in a particular country.

The patience to hear others can potentially help a particular individual and human being play a constructive role in the conflict resolution. It is also important to focus on a particular conflict only before getting into any other conflict or controversy. It means that the conflict resolution has to go on gradually and sequentially as compared to taking on a multitasking approach. The seeking of mutually agreed approach has to be floated by the affected parties, and individuals within a conflict ended situation. This can ultimately help the individuals encountered with a particular conflict find out an appropriate and agreeable conflict resolution scenario to get out of the challenging situation ultimate.

TECHNIQUE 31: TRACK EATING, SLEEPING, AND WORKING PATTERNS

❖ **Explore this question:** What does eating, sleeping, and working patterns of a person tell us about his personality?

The eating, sleeping, and working patterns of a person tell a lot about his personality. Juliet Boghossian, a behavioral food expert, illustrates that food and eating habits can potentially help in the estimation and evaluation of a particular individual's personality. The different personalities can be associated with the different levels of the eating habits adopted by individuals. The food-specific habits of a particular individual can help in the exploration and evolution of the different facets and the personality-oriented characteristics of a particular individual. The behavioral tendencies related to the food-specific habits and eating of an individual can reflect a particular personality type acquired by that particular individual.

1. The slow eaters usually like to be the people who want to remain in control, and they like to appreciate their life-oriented activities. There is a possibility that some of the people with slow eating abilities tend to feel pressurized as compared to the cutting speed of the other people around. They are capable of enjoying their food more as compared to the other types of eaters.

2. The fast eaters may be potentially the people who earn more ambitious and only oriented within their lives. They usually try to catch up with different things within a specified range of the time which clearly indicates their

ambitiousness to achieve certain targets.

3. The isolationist and picky people, with respect to their eating habits, may be completely different in their personalities as they tend to lead more sequential actual lives. They usually tend to come out with different sorts of personality-oriented characteristics and lifestyle as compared to the other types of people with different eating habits.

The personality analysis, in the light of the eating habits, can be further integrated and connected with the sleeping as well as the word printed approach adopted by the individuals in their real life. The bottom line can be to look at the possibility related to the sleeping as well as the eating habits of an individual with the acceleration of certain characteristics of its personality. The comprehensive and in-depth analysis in the eating, as well as sleeping, behavior of individuals can help in the exploration of certain personality-oriented dynamics and the behaviors which they are more likely to exhibit in their real lives.

TECHNIQUE 32: DETECT AND EXAMINE WAYS OF EXPRESSING INNER TURMOIL AND PROFOUND THINKING

What is Inner Turmoil?

It's an emotional condition when a person is bound in self fears, hate, disgust, etc. It is the state in which a person is stressed out and self-pity himself. He feels agitated and confused. He starts self-torturing himself. No one gets into this depressing situation by choice, but some external factor makes the brain to behave like that.

Types of Inner Turmoil

There are certain types of turmoil's happens due to some specific situation.

1) Principled turmoil
2) Religious turmoil
3) Breakup turmoil
4) Low self-esteem turmoil

The Correlation between Internal and External Turmoil

Internal turmoil is the conflict going on inside an individual. It's a fight between the inner emotions of the person and the external turmoil of the other persons or objects which creates panic and conflicts. They both can be interlinked because, most of the time, internal turmoil takes place due to the external turmoil. The major difference between the two is that inner turmoil cannot be seen, but the external turmoil is clearly visible if observed carefully.

How People Express Inner Turmoil

When it comes to getting rid of the internal turmoil or express their profound thinking, people adopt various ways in order to help get away with conflicting emotions running inside their minds. It's difficult to get out of your profound thinking, but it is only possible when the specific individual truly wants to come out from the traumatized state. There are numerous ways, but some are mentioned below:

By Talking

Talking to someone you are emotionally attached to will help you to get rid of that inner turmoil faster than you can imagine. Stress levels decrease when you share your emotions and know that the person you are conveying your emotions understands and feels your emotions well. And eventually, the words of comfort from that particular person gives a feeling of contentment.

By Being Creative

Rather than talking and sharing their emotions with someone, most people with inner turmoil opt for being creative. It can be anything like making paintings, creating artifacts, writing a good poem, etc. All these creative activities help a person with a turbulent mental state to feel better and relaxed. It acts as a catharsis for them.

By Exercising

It is rare, but there are people who take out themselves from inner turmoil by exercising. It can be jogging, weight training, Zumba, or any physical activity that can take them out from their mental stress in a manner that they feel lighter both physically and mentally.

By Watching Comedy Theatre

When getting out of inner turmoil, people also prefer to

attend a good theatre program. Mostly, they opt for a comedy movie just to give themselves a good laugh and positivity.

By Relaxing with Animals and Nature

Animals can also act as your anti-depressant. Yes, it's true; some people find peace in nature and animals. They prefer to go into someplace nearer to nature or spend some time with their pets to bring back their minds on track.

By Sleeping

There is this strange habit in some people which, for them, sleep acts as a delete button. They put everything on a back burner and grab some hours of deep sleep to relax and refresh. When they wake up again, they often have already forgotten or eliminated the disturbing thoughts from their minds. Long and comfortable sleep makes them feel light-headed and full of regained energy for the day ahead.

❖ Bonus Question to Explore:

What do time management, future planning, goals, and leisure activities of a person tells us about his personality?

The time management and future planning skills and associated behavior of a particular person clearly indicate that his personality gets influenced by these change agents and behavior patterns. To perform the adequate level of personality analysis, you must explore these sorts of customized questions and brainstorm investigative ideas to come up with suitable, complementary information about a person's personality traits. There are different personality types that can be classified on the basis of looking at the time management skills of a particular individual. For instance:

1. The Time Martyrs: An individual who is more inclined towards focusing on spending time on behalf of others as compared to managing the time for itself may belong to this category of the time management personality type

2. The Wild Procrastinators: The procrastination can be potentially perceived as the opposite of productivity. It clearly means that Wild Procrastinators are the individuals who are not capable of managing the time in the best way to

enhance the level of the productivity and his struggle to achieve their life specific objectives as a whole

3.   The Underestimators: These are the people that are usually underestimating the worth of their time responding to a particular task or project-specific accomplishment. The mistake regarding the estimation of the right time to complete a particular task of a project result in a negative way for them.

4.   The Do-It-Alls: These are the individuals who try to focus on managing their activities in accordance with time. They try to give out the maximum level of productivity in order to perform the maximum level of the work in a given time duration.

5.   The   Commitment Phobes: The   free spirited individuals usually focus on the level of the commitment more than the content of the constructive part of a particular project or task assigned to them. It means that in these personality types, you will be focused on the utilization of the time in accordance with their particular moods.

Similarly, the leisure activities of a person also help in the identification of its particular personality. The hobbies and leisure activities can be combined with the time management and the futuristic planning-oriented abilities of individuals in order to find out the personality type precisely. The Do-It-Alls type personality may be considered as one of the best personality type looking at time management skills and the future planning abilities of the individuals. This type of personality can provide a particular individual with an ability to become more productive and objective with respect to the achievement of adequate objectives set within its lifestyle. There are still some of the characteristics associated with this particular most productive type of human personality responding to time management skills as it is not possible for a person to become 100% productive all the time. There should be a work-life balance in order to provide the individual with an ability to accomplish its tasks precisely and accurately.

CHAPTER 10: EMOTIONAL INTELLIGENCE AND PERSONALITY ANALYSIS

Sometimes lack of emotional IQ, simply known as EQ, also creates complications for efficient communication. An emotionally immature person will not be able to communicate well the way a person who is emotionally mature enough can do. An emotionally intelligent person can handle the situations calmly and peacefully.

TECHNIQUE 33

✓ Look into yourself, track your personality traits.

✓ Understand empathy vs. sympathy.

✓ Put yourself in other's shoes. See, are you emotionally intelligent?

Intelligence can be measured in quotients. Most of us are familiar with the word IQ, which is intelligence quotients, in which our ability to memorize and logical reasoning is checked and EQ is emotional quotients in which persons handling of emotions in adversity are observed. Emotional intelligence is to recognize and understand other people's emotion or to stay calm and think sensibly during a panic situation.

Traits of Emotional Intelligence

Mentioned below are some qualities of a person having high emotional intelligence quotient:

Sympathy + Empathy Combination

On top of the list is the trait which shows kindness towards others. One with the kind heart and bright soul can think about others, and sometimes, even put himself in others' place as well in order to realize his state of mind. Generally, a person with good EQ thinks more about others than himself. A more detailed debate on sympathy vs. empathy will be discussed separately.

Self-Recognition

If a person understands himself well, he will be able to perform his responsibilities in a better way than the person who still doesn't realize his actual worth. It is necessary to keep analyzing yourself to improve and enhance yourself for a better life ahead.

Inquisitive Nature & Investigative Mind

An inquisitive person gets success easily because of his passion and curiosity to learn and grow. He observes his surroundings works with the curious mind thus gets what he wants in a minimum amount of time.

The most emotionally intelligent people are those who work with an investigative mind. They always keep analyzing the information which comes in their path. They try to keep moving their mind in a manner to observe their habits and try to improve them in an efficient way.

Self Belief

You can't do anything if you don't believe in yourself. It's about self- control. Controlling your emotions is working with peace of mind. Once you start believing that everything happens for a reason, things get easy for survival. Hard work and a positive attitude are the key factors of a person's success. Doing meditation also makes your belief in yourself without any doubts.

Control on Desires

It's the best characteristic of an emotionally intelligent person that he doesn't get confused with the needs and wants. He stays focused and prefers to fulfill the needs first rather than the desires. It helps him set his priorities, thus making him focus on the actual goals of life.

Dedication

A true element present in an emotionally intelligent person is the dedication and his passion for his work, relations, and goals. He gives his best to get the maximum out of his efforts. Without dedication, no one can achieve the desired results.

Positive Approach

If an individual wants a steady success in life, then he must have to be optimistic about the things around him. He should build a positive attitude around himself so that no external element can destroy his focus.

Versatility & Adaptability

An emotionally intelligent person believes in versatility. He knows when to stop and when to indulge in some particular work or relation. He believes in adapting to situations in a positive manner and try to behave accordingly. He knows that adaptability is the quality which makes not only his life comfortable but others' too.

Empathy vs. Sympathy

Do you want satisfying and deep relations? You have to understand the difference between empathy and sympathy.

❖ **Empathy:** It is an ability to understand the feelings of other people. Remember, empathy can fuel connections.

❖ **Sympathy:** It allows you to become a part of other's feelings. To drive connections, humans need compassion.

These are confusing terms in English, and people often use them interchangeably, as synonyms. Remember, these are related, but different words. Here is a brief explanation to understand the meaning and use of these words.

Sympathy (Seeing & Feeling)

Sympathy means concern or displaying caring emotions for someone. These emotions often come along with a wish to see him/her happy. It implies a sense of sharing similarities with profound engagement. Under this shared feeling, you can feel compassion, pity, or sorrow for others.

For instance, if your friend loses her father or any other loved one, you will feel sympathy for him/her and their family. In this situation, people can express this feeling with sadness. It can be difficult to feel empathy for this loss without having the same experience in your life.

Greeting cards with flowers for mourning families are sympathy cards. It means you have harmony with sufferers. Remember, feelings of sympathy for an organization are support, loyalty, and approval.

Empathy (Feeling & Understanding)

You can share and recognize the emotions of other people or even a fictional character. Empathy is an emotion that is stronger than sympathy. If you can put yourself in the same situation to understand the intensity of sadness or happiness of another person, it is empathy.

For instance, you are the kind of person who can't understand the feelings of another person unless you imagine yourself in his place. You have empathy if you can put yourself in a similar situation and perceive the feelings of another individual. Unfortunately, people often confuse empathy with compassion, sympathy, or pity.

If you are feeling uncomfortable seeing someone in a distressing or depressing situation, you are feeling pity. This emotion is less engaging than compassion, sympathy, or empathy. Empathy allows you to open up your senses and let the situation affect you in a way that you feel yourself responding to the call of emotions. It is challenging to feel empathetic without facing a similar situation in your life.

Right Time to Use the Term "Empathy"

Empathy allows you to identify and understand the feelings or situations of others. For instance, you can follow the condition of a homeless family because a cyclone once demolished your house. If you can put yourself in another's situation, the word empathy is right for you. Empathy is a noun, and for the very first time, it was used in 1895. This tells us that people started becoming emotionally intelligent back then.

Right Time to Use the Term "Sympathy"

Sympathy (again a noun) was used for the very first time in the 1500s. If you have feelings of pity or grief, you are showing solidarity. For instance, you can show sympathy to a grieving mother because, even though you have not experienced this situation yourself, you have a sensitive personality that lets you feel for others. Your personality traits include feelings such as kindness, generosity, care, and compassion.

Empathy means you are identifying another person's sorrow as your own. Therefore, you will be willing to walk the extra mile to support and protect that person as if you were doing that for yourself in a similar situation. Putting yourself in someone else's shoes will not only make you feel bad about a grieving person but make you want to make some positive changes as well to improve his situation. Suppose, you are looking at your friend while he tells you his emotional experience, a painful tale of past grievances. You are analyzing his expressions and sub-textual emotions while he speaks, and you notice his eyes well up. If you are an emotionally intelligent person having a high EQ rate, you would feel for his sorrow and the extent of his grief almost instantly. Maybe you would not even have to go as far as processing each word of his narrative to reach on a conclusion that he seeks support and empathy. Just looking at his tearful eyes, you may as well feel your eyes becoming teary.

Sometimes, sympathizing and saying sorry is not enough. Sometimes, a person does not just need a shoulder to cry on, and a pat on the back as consolation that everything would be fine. Sometimes, they just want you to cry with them instead of wiping their tears. Sometimes, you just need to let the flood gates open and get rid of all the accumulated debris and emotional baggage in order to feel lighthearted.

CONCLUSION

Thank you for making it through to the end of How to Analyze People and Understand the Human Mind. Let's hope it was informative and able to provide you with all of the tools you need to achieve your goals whatever they may be.

The next step is to transition from the book-practice to real-life practicum. The experiences are what make us into what we are today. After reading about the human personality analysis and people-reading with speed and quality methods, you are better equipped with the tools and techniques necessary to understand people and interact with them effectively. This is your chance to go out there and start proving your worth by not only differentiating your friends from your foes but also by turning the threat of failure into an opportunity for success. No longer should you fumble around with words to say in front of a stranger, or let misunderstandings ruin your relationships. Don't let people or environmental factors get the best of your efforts and well-intendedness nor let your misguided observation or judgmental views get the best of the good wishes of people around you. Look into their personality, try to understand their behavior, explore the possibilities, and analyze their intentions. This will help you in not only sustaining the old relationships along with building the new ones but also let you get successful by remaining one step ahead of your opponents.

Although we admit that the subject of human behavioral psychology is every vast, no way can it be summed up on a limited range of pages. However, we did try our best to accumulate the most sought after and relevant techniques that are easy to understand and focus more on action than mere wordiness so that they can be learned and implemented right away.

Finally, if you found this book useful in any way, a review on Amazon is always appreciated!

INFORMATION ABOUT THE PUBLISHER

The self-help book publisher is a book publisher. With almost 10 years of experience in the self-help niche, he has published the best books through his writers. Follow our publications to embark on the journey of personal growth.

Follow our website, www.selfhelpbookpublisher.org, to discover new updates and publications.

Made in the USA
San Bernardino, CA
18 May 2020